Help, I'm Stuck!

10 Mistakes Christian Women Make

When Pursuing Their Purpose

By Dexter and Tiffany Godfrey

http://www.RelationshipMissionaries.com

Help, I'm Stuck!

10 Mistakes Christian Women Make

When Pursuing Their Purpose

Unless otherwise noted, Scriptures are taken from the New King James Bible (NKJV), copyright 1999 by Thomas Nelson, Inc.

Published by Leadership and Sales Academy

Printed in the United States of America

ISBN: 978-0-9862003-1-1

SPECIAL DISCLAIMER

The authors and publisher shall in no event be held liable for any loss or other damages, including but not limited to special, incidental, consequential, or other damages. The authors and publisher of this material have used their best efforts in preparing this book. The authors and publisher make no representation or warranties with respect to the accuracy, applicability, fitness, or completeness of the contents of this program. All links and resources are for informational purposes only and are not warranted for content, accuracy or any other implied explicit purpose. They disclaim any warranties (expressed or implied), merchantability, or fitness for any particular purpose.

No single book of life purpose advice can be used as a substitute for professional, personalized advice. Readers are encouraged to seek advice from qualified professionals, including licensed counselors, pastors, coaches, and other qualified individuals.

This report contains material protected under International and Federal Copyright Laws and Treaties. Any unauthorized reprint or use of this material is prohibited without the express, written permission of the authors or publisher.

Because you bought our book, we'd like to invite you to take advantage of our **One-time ZERO COST** 'Rapid Impact' Coaching Session so you can discover the benefits of pursuing your purpose.

It all starts with building a strong foundation on God's love for you.

If you want to create your own life strategy for finding your purpose, then here's what you can do:

You can email us at info@RelationshipMissionaries.com to request your FREE coaching session.

Use the subject line: "Coaching Session – STUCK!"

Or

Visit http://relationshipmissionaries.com/find-purpose-today/

Fill out the form and we will follow up with you shortly.

During this 20-minute session, you will get a bird's eye view of your purpose and so you can get on track with the plan God has for your life.

Do it today because your purpose won't wait forever!

DEDICATION

This book is dedicated to our sons, HJ and Chase, their future wives, and to every woman who is hungry and will do whatever it takes to pursue her purpose.

You are significant to God and unconditionally loved by Him.

Today, begin your journey with Him as He holds your hand and enables you to step into your purpose with boldness and confidence in Him.

ACKNOWLEDGMENTS

Our Parents: Had it not been for your support over the course of our lives, we would be different people. Thank you for shaping and molding us and then releasing us to become who God called us to be! We love you.

The Leary Family: Thank you for all the support, both in person and online.

The Godfrey Family: Thank you for your love and the stories you've shared.

The Holden Family: Thanks for your love and acts of love. You are the real deal, family!

The Edwards Family: Thanks for the lessons you've shared on paper, online, on the phone, and in person. Your love and support have been indescribable.

Thanks to these church families who helped us to find our purpose and voice in the Body of Christ:

- Bishop Courtney and Pastor Janeen McBath, and the Calvary Revival Church Family

- Pastor Hendricks and the Faith Baptist Church Family

- Pastor Rylander and the New Mount Olive Baptist Church Family

- Bishop Robert Hargrove and the Cathedral Grace Family Church

- Pastor Jerome Barber and the Sixth Mount Zion Baptist Temple Church Family

Thanks for all the great teaching, support, and encouragement you've shown us over the years.

Special thanks to:

Family Life, Keith and Trish Tully, and the Williamsburg/Richmond Weekend to Remember Team who confirmed the call of God on our lives to minister in the area of relationships.

The JMT family who has always shown support and encouraged us to move forward.

To countless other family and friends who have helped us along the way as we've strived to put God's heart for people in writing and onto paper.

Our readers who encourage us to keep writing and speaking life to those around us.

Our social media followers who offer us thoughts and ideas that need to be addressed in writing. We want to offer you solutions so you can pursue your purpose.

TABLE OF CONTENTS

Introduction...i

Mistake #1: All Dressed Up and No Place to Go.…...1

Mistake #2: He Loves Me, He Loves Me Not! 20

Mistake #3: It's Too Dark in Here! 35

Mistake #4: I'm Too Busy for That! 49

Mistake #5: Ouch, That Hurt!................................. 68

Mistake #6: Push It! 86

Mistake #7: Girls, Girls, Girls! 101

Mistake #8: Thanks for What? 117

Chapter 9: Oops! I Miscounted............................ 129

Chapter 10: Tag, You're It! 145

Conclusion 161

Meet Dexter and Tiffany Godfrey 167

Additional Resources by Dexter and Tiffany 170

INTRODUCTION

Hello, Friend:

Have you ever felt stuck?

We are Dexter and Tiffany Godfrey.

As trainers and life coaches, we've had the opportunity to help countless people like you who wanted more out of life and to discover their purpose for living.

During our training and coaching sessions, we realized many of these people constantly seek to find their meaning and reason for living.

While our coaching and training have helped them in many ways, there are so many women we will never meet. However, we truly believe that women just like you can benefit from some of the tips, questions, and challenges we have offered our current and past clients. For this reason, we created this book as your personal life coaching guide, which will help you to navigate your way to your purpose and destiny.

Use this book to catapult you into your purpose.

Here's why -- **God loves you so much!**

He pursues you on a daily basis! (We'll prove it to you later in this book.)

God wants to communicate with you every day and He wants to include you in His plans for His glory and your greatness.

He has a plan for you based on your passions, skills, gifts, and life experience (both good and bad).

And the good news is that He wants you to get started on the path to your purpose right now!

As life purpose coaches, our only goal is to encourage you to get unstuck by helping you to move forward and work toward consistent change and growth.

Unlike a counselor, who takes a person back to their past to help them find healing, our job as life purpose coaches is to help you see where you currently are in relation to where you want to ultimately be. Through a series of thought-provoking questions we can guide you to develop a strategic plan for a pathway to your purpose and discovering your "Why," or the reason why God created you to live on this earth.

What We'll Cover:

We will talk to you about your purpose based on God's blueprint for your life.

Guess what? **You were created for a purpose long before you were born**[t1].

We're going to dive into the core of your being by helping you discover who you really are and who you were created to become.

You were created to pursue God and enjoy a relationship with Him. Through your relationship, you give Him the honor and attention (glory) He deserves.

To do this and to help you discover your purpose, we'll ask you some open-ended coaching questions throughout this book. The goal of these questions is to help you to look at where you are, consider where you are going, and give you the tools you'll need to get there.

In Habakkuk 2:2, God told Habakkuk to write his vision (a goal, or a picture of where he believed God wanted him to be in life) so he could carry it out.

We want you to read this book and grab the tips we share, so you can do the same as Habakkuk.

To get started on this journey to your vision, we recommend you get a notebook and a pen while reading this book so you can take some notes. Doing this will enable you to eventually create a clear cut vision for your life.

This book will help you to learn about your purpose. In fact, we'll give you a taste...[t2]

We will also look at the lives of some prominent visionaries from the Bible. Many people often trivialize the people in the Bible as if they are the characters of a fictitious story.

However, God placed the life stories of these people in His book to show how His extraordinary power works in the lives of ordinary people who pursued Him with all their hearts.

Now our question to you is, "Are you willing to pursue God so He can do extraordinary things in and through you?"

What is your purpose?

Your purpose is your "Why," or your reason for doing what we do.

As Christians, our ultimate purpose is to bring honor and attention to God and draw others to Him.

We connect with God by understanding and receiving His love for us. Then as we come to better understand God and His desires, we will learn what it takes to fulfill this purpose as we discover our gifts, skills, and life story.

However, when we don't have a strong relationship with God because we don't spend time with Him, we won't get the proper guidance we need. As a result, we often find ourselves lost and searching for direction.

And the crazy thing is we often think we're okay, but we soon find ourselves "stuck."

Have you ever been there?

Are you there now?

Biggest Mistake Women Make in Pursuing Their Purpose:

Remember earlier when we said that **God loves you** and He wants to spend time with you?

It's true.

Jeremiah 31:3 says that God loves you with an everlasting love and with that same love He has drawn you.

Trust us when we tell you: **God is in hot pursuit of you!**

He wants you more than any other man. And He can fulfill the empty, dark places of your heart if you let Him.

But the problem is that many women don't realize God's unconditional love for them.

In fact, we would say this is the biggest mistake women make in trying to figure out their purpose.

When we don't have a revelation (a discovery or uncovering) of God's love for us, we don't see Him as a priority.

Instead, God becomes nothing more than a distant Supreme Being who is all-powerful, yet only cares about the "important people" and the "emergencies" in our lives.

And when we fail to see God as a loving Friend, Father, and Confidant, we don't recognize that He is a present Person who is concerned about everything (even a hangnail!)

And we will say it again: **God loves you!**

He loves you when you are good, bad, or even just plain crazy.

And guess what?

He even loves you on a bad hair day and even when your clothes don't fit right.

We could go on and on about how much God loves you, but until you come to recognize this for yourself, our words won't matter.

Our hope is that you will receive and embrace God's love and connect with Him on a deeper level than you do now.

Then we want to encourage you to allow God to patiently walk you toward the destiny He has for you.

How This Book is Different:

Most books fill your head with the "YOU' factor:

- How YOU can find your purpose
- How YOU can do whatever you want
- How YOU can get whatever you want
- How YOU can use your gifts
- How YOU can create a new you.

They often stress "YOU."

But the problem with "YOU" (and each one of us) is that without God, we are ineffective, or at best limited. We can only go so far in becoming who God wants us to be without Him. In fact, John 15:5 says without Him we can do nothing.

This book is also jam-packed with thought-provoking questions that will help you to discover who you are so you can get closer to recognizing your purpose and how you can help others. You don't need to have the perfect answer for each question.

You don't have to answer each question immediately. You may need to take some time to think, mediate (ponder) and look to God for insight first. That's okay because your answer will come in God's timing.

While this book is filled with practical principles and suggestions for growth, anything you attempt to do can only be done successfully by the grace and mercy of Christ.

With this being said, other books focus on how you have to wait and wish to see what your purpose will become.

This book is different.

Some would argue that focusing on mistakes is being negative. I disagree.

When you watch for the pitfalls to avoid and you learn and recognize the traps ahead of time, you can save a lot of time, frustration, money, and heartache.

Plus, as humans, we often learn by example.

In other words, we can learn from others people's mistakes without making the same ones.

And when it comes to something as important as pursuing your purpose, you can't afford to take one second longer than necessary to start getting results.

So let's stop wasting time and let me show you how to avoid each and every one of these 10 mistakes Christian women make when pursuing their purpose.

MISTAKE #1: ALL DRESSED UP AND NO PLACE TO GO…

"But ye are a chosen generation, a royal priesthood, an holy nation, a peculiar people; that ye should shew forth the praises of him who hath called you out of darkness into his marvelous light…" 1 Peter 2:9 (KJV)

What is the mistake?

Not knowing your purpose.

This mistake happens when people don't understand their purpose but instead live aimlessly, without recognizing they were created by God for a specific reason.

Many Christian women live their lives frustrated, overwhelmed, and confused about life. Although they have accepted Christ as their Savior, they still feel a sense of emptiness, a void that needs to be filled.

They may work their 9-5 corporate jobs or stay home taking care of their children, but they're not satisfied. They want more, but often don't know where to start.

They feel they were created to do more, be more, and ultimately become who God created them to be.

So in an attempt to fulfill the void, they attend conferences, read books, become more active in church, and get involved in relationships (which may or may not be healthy for them), among other things.

While there's nothing wrong with learning more and getting good information for personal there's good news and bad news about this.

We'll start with the bad news. These attempts to find fulfillment may not always be the answer to what they are looking for.

The good news is that God does have more for these women. He has more for you. But let's look at the mistake a lot of Christian women make.

Simply stated, this mistake occurs when a woman believes she can meander through life and take up space without any real focus or goals. This is far from the truth.

It's sad because God has equipped and dressed us with purpose, but many of us don't know where to go or how to begin.

What is purpose?

Your purpose is your "Why," the reason why God created you and why you are living on this earth. You were born at the right time, the right location, and will meet the right people to help you to accomplish your purpose in life.

You were created to pursue God and enjoy a relationship with Him. Through your relationship, you give God the honor and glory (attention), He deserves, while you make a difference in the lives of those around you.

You make this difference as you take advantage of the gifts and skills God gives you, as well the experiences He allows you to go through.

God has a purpose for each one of us, and He uses everything, both the good and the bad, to get us closer to our purpose (Romans 8:28).

However, when a woman doesn't recognize her purpose, she tends to miss out on the abundant life God promises by randomly picking something and doing it without recognizing the gifts, talents, and experiences God has placed inside of her.

This woman may have an idea that she was born for a specific reason, but she often doesn't know how to figure it out.

We've learned that people often try to find their call or purpose through other people. Ironically, this method of finding purpose is misleading because most people don't even know their own purpose!

These people will give you the wrong advice that could ultimately hurt you and cause you to waste a lot of precious time. And while people will never admit to it, they often find it easier to tell you what you should do with your life versus seeking God to learn and discover their own purpose.

These well-meaning "counselors" offer both solicited and unsolicited advice, but they are often unqualified[3] and ill-equipped to guide you in the right direction for your life.

Why is it a mistake?

When you don't know your purpose, you won't recognize your significance to the world and the people around you. When you don't think you're significant or valuable enough, you won't do anything to make as much of a difference for the Kingdom of God or to touch the lives of other individuals. You can also miss out on valuable opportunities for growth.

What's worse, you will constantly find yourself frustrated because you're not walking in your purpose or operating in your gifts. Then when you see another person doing what you were created to do, you may even become angry, envious, and jealous of them because they obeyed the call, but you didn't.

One of the saddest things of not fully understanding your purpose is that this lack of direction can lead you to just "settling" in various areas of your life. You can run the risk of experiencing good things in life, but not ultimately God's best for your life.

This type of thinking can lead you to a cycle of going through the motions in life: Go to work, go to church, go home, and cook dinner. Go to work, go to church, go home, and cook dinner. Go to... You know where I'm going with this!

Going through the motions becomes a mundane, boring, and fruitless life in which you only exist to live and please others. As a result, you never realize that God had a more abundant life for you to live.

While it's important to take care of your family, minister to others, go to work, go to church, etc., we often can get into a rut that only leads to us leaving God out and performing as robots, based on the demands of our day.

God is no longer the focal point, and you are not walking in the purpose He has called you to. God wants to be a part of our daily lives, and calls us to be fruitful on a consistent basis. He wants us to be aware of His presence and love for us. He calls us to righteousness, peace, and joy in the Holy Ghost (Romans 14:17).

How can we do this if we just live life with no purpose or assurance of His guidance and presence in our lives?

What are the consequences of making this mistake and how critical are they?

The consequences of making this mistake are extremely critical because when you don't recognize your value and purpose, you will become vulnerable to the enemy's traps and deception.

Since you don't recognize your value, it becomes easy to allow the devil to carry you on a journey of confusion, frustration, unnecessary drama, complacency, or even sin.

You will also live on the earth without fulfilling your purpose or leaving a godly legacy for your family and those around you that is not as great as it could have been.

The frustration you have as a result of this could lead you to bitterness and resentment because you aren't truly doing what God created you to do. And you could spend your life complaining and making other people's lives miserable because you're dissatisfied with life.

For example, imagine you purchase an expensive tube of lipstick with the intent of wearing it to a special event. But if your children used that same lipstick to paint the walls or color a picture, it's not being used for its main purpose.

This leaves you frustrated, disappointed, and I dare say, angry!

Why? Because the lipstick was expensive and valuable to you, but the purpose was devalued and minimized because your children didn't recognize the true value or intent of the lipstick.

When you don't understand your value and refuse to fulfill God's intended purpose for your life, God is not mad with you, but He is expecting a return on the investment He made in you.

With this in mind, beloved, God gave you your value even before you were born, and He knew exactly who He created you to become (Jeremiah 1:5). That value, since it was given to you by your Creator, cannot be taken away by your "where," unless you allow it to be taken away.

It's so important to know your "who" (the great value God created you to be), and your "where" (your circumstances, mistakes, weaknesses, shortcomings, or the opinions of others). Unfortunately, we sometimes allow our "where" to define us, but your "where" will always give you a lesser value than what you are worth.

Remember that where you are in life is not who you are because who you are in life is always greater than where you are. Your "who" is defined by Christ, not circumstances! And if you allow Him, He will determine your "where" because He has a great plan and purpose for your life (Jeremiah 29:11).

Why and when do women tend to make this mistake?

While many women grew up in the church, they didn't understand God's plan and purpose for their lives because in many cases nobody taught them.

For instance, it wasn't until later in life that we understood that God created us for a specific purpose.

In fact, a lot of women may not even understand God's love for them or His personal concern for their lives.

Many women also never discovered how to recognize their gifts, talents, and abilities, and they do not see the importance of honing their skills. While they may be good at a few things, they take these skills, gifts, and abilities for granted, but never recognize them as a solution to someone else's problem.

For this reason, they don't develop themselves to the fullest because they don't see the connection between what they do and the purpose God has for their lives.

Another reason why women tend to make this mistake is because they suffer from insecurity, and they want to feel validated by others. As a result, they would rather "play it safe" by staying in a box, following the crowd, and listening to advice from their friends, even if the advice is incorrect and detrimental to their future.

While the world might want you to fit in, God wants you to stand out.

Let us tell you a quick story to illustrate this point.

I, (Tiffany) have wanted to be a writer, pretty much all of my life.

I would share my stories with a lot of people, including family, friends, and colleagues in my area of work, only for them to say, "Oh, that's nice," or, "How are you going to make money as a writer?"

I would attend writer's conferences and writer's groups to connect with other like-minded individuals, and while this did help me to some extent, no one ever asked to publish my writings during those times.

I often became disheartened with my life because I didn't know who could help me to get published. And for a while I even gave up on my dream of writing when life sent a series of circumstances that hit hard.

But eventually, I came back to my writing and I took time to find my niche, or area of expertise. I began to discover how my words could really make a difference in the lives of certain individuals, particularly hurt and broken women.

I also took time to learn more about myself and examine why I kept hitting so many obstacles with my writing. This required me to look at myself -- the good, the bad, and the ugly!

This self-examination wasn't easy, but I pressed forward anyway.

It required me to spend time in God's Word, seeking Him, and allowing Him to lead me. After much time, prayer, and thought, I recognized that I was put on this earth to coach, teach, train, and help women to build healthy relationships.

I finally fulfilled my dream of writing and publishing books, but God had something bigger in mind.

Then I began to connect with the right people who would carry me to my next level of recognizing my true purpose of adding value to relationships through speaking, coaching, and team building.

While spending time in prayer, seeking God, waiting to hear from Him, and learning to discover what He wanted me to do, was not easy, I can tell you that it was worth the process.

I encourage you to never shortcut the process no matter how long it takes and never, ever give up on the dreams you believe God has placed in your heart!

What Questions Should You Consider?

Questions to consider...

- Does God have a purpose for me?

- If so, what is it?

- What do I really have a passion for?

- What excites me?

- What makes me angry?

- What injustices do I see?

- What can I do to solve these injustices?

- In what areas have I failed and overcome?

- Who are some people in my life that seem to know their purpose and can offer me sound, godly, advice?

What should you do if you've already made this mistake? How do you fix it?

If you've already fallen into this trap, here's how you get out...

Spend some time in the presence of God. This involves studying His Word, prayer, meditating on Scripture, journaling, and worship. We'll talk about this in more detail later in the book.

Right now, just give yourself some time to think and hear the voice of God.

Consider areas of ministry and/or work where you have participated in and have experienced a level of success. While I often felt like a failure in so many areas of my life, I did recognize that I had success in my marriage and other relationships.

Bingo! Relationships would become my area of expertise and my place of purpose.

Think about yourself. Consider what gifts, abilities, and skills come naturally to you.

In what areas do you consider yourself experienced or knowledgeable? In what areas do people ask you for advice?

Stop interacting and spending a lot of time with friends who are negative and don't understand God's purpose for their own lives. Negative people can talk you out of the very thing that God has equipped and called you to do.

For this reason, it's important to find people who encourage you in love, and hold you accountable in pursuing your purpose so you can stay on track.

How do we prevent making this mistake moving forward?

Here's what you should do to prevent this mistake from happening moving forward...

* Read Habakkuk 2:2, which says "Write the vision and make it plain…"

* Write down Scripture that speaks about purpose. In addition to Habakkuk 2, a good place to start would be Jeremiah 1:5. In this passage, God tells Jeremiah

as a young boy that He has called him for a specific purpose. And just like Jeremiah, God has called you for a specific purpose.

- Write down the type of people you can envision yourself helping. For instance, is it single parents, married couples, widows, women who are making a career change, or college kids who are trying to find their place in the world?

- Start reading books that focus on purpose. One book that helped me was *The Purpose Driven Life* by Rick Warren. There are many others out there.

- Once you discover your purpose (or at least have an idea of your purpose), create a 20-word purpose statement. This is a clear succinct way of expressing your purpose. You will use this as a guideline as you work to get to your purpose. Getting it down to 20 words may take some time. For instance, you may start out writing a 50-word statement, but as you keep looking at it, you can decide what can be taken out. Eventually you can get it down to 20 words.

Action steps for this chapter:

Based on my experience, here's some insight that can really help you with this issue...

Write a list of the following things:

- Your passions
- Lessons learned
- Abilities
- Work experience
- Ministry
- Volunteer experiences
- Good and bad experiences
- Strengths/weaknesses
- Things you possess that can take you to your next level
- Network/groups you have access to

I suggest you categorize these items.

Complete this list within the next three days. Look over your list and consider how you can use all of these things to fulfill your purpose.

Our BIGGEST piece of advice moving forward...

[t4]Refuse to waste time thinking that you're here on Earth to take up space. God has a specific plan for your life and He's waiting on you to fulfill it, so get started today!

Summary:

- God created you for a specific purpose.

- If you don't fulfill your purpose, your frustration can lead you to bitterness and resentment toward others.

- Recognize that your value was given to you by your Creator and no person or set of circumstances can take that value away.

- Take some quiet time to consider what God wants you to do.

- Read, write down, meditate, and journal on some Scriptures about God's purpose for your life.

- Create a list of your assets, experiences, skills, and other characteristics within three days so you can analyze what direction to take in pursuing your purpose.

Now that we've covered how to avoid the CURRENT MISTAKE, it's time to move on to how to get the NEXT MISTAKE[t5].

MISTAKE #2: HE LOVES ME, HE LOVES ME NOT!

"The LORD has appeared of old to me, *saying:* "Yes, I have loved you with an everlasting love; Therefore with lovingkindness I have drawn you." Jeremiah 31:3

What is the mistake?

Not recognizing how much God loves you.

This mistake occurs when women do not understand or recognize God's love for them.

Instead, they often base God's love for them on their past and present circumstances.

They also base God's love on their hurtful relationships with other people, including their fathers, ex-boyfriends, ex-husbands, and even their current spouses.

For instance, when a father is not present in a girl's life, this image often travels with her throughout her relationships with other people. She struggles with her self-esteem and often finds it difficult to receive and give love from others because she feels it was never demonstrated to her.

Since a father's love is often associated with God, if a woman has daddy issues, she will find it hard to relate to God as her Father. And worse, she won't clearly understand God's love for her unless she takes time to dig deep to discover the truth of His unconditional love specifically for her.

Why is it a mistake?

This is a mistake because believing that God does not love you is far from the truth!

This lie is the enemy's way of trying to discourage women from having a viable, loving relationship with God.

When a woman doesn't recognize God's unconditional love for her, she could settle for anything in life.

It's also a mistake because it causes her to look for love from everyone and everywhere else except God. Because she doesn't feel genuine love from anyone else, this can lead to unfulfilling and unsatisfying relationships that can become toxic and ultimately pull her away from her purpose.

What are the consequences of making this mistake and how critical are they?

When you don't understand God's love for you, it can lead you to believe lies about God. You could begin to view God as a Judge, who's just waiting to condemn you. In addition, you could run from God, although He's reaching out to love you and walk with you on your journey.

You may even believe that God is mad at you, but He's not. He's actually a loving God who's ready to embrace and bless you.

If you do not understand God's love, you could struggle to experience a deep, true relationship with God because He could seem like a distant, uncaring prison warden.

In addition, if you continue to allow the enemy to discourage you from experiencing a relationship with God and receiving His love, you could become indifferent to God's goodness. As a result, you will dismiss God, and ultimately give credit to yourself when good things happen.

Or you will view every blessing you receive as a "mere coincidence," and this will cause you to become prideful and never fully experience the goodness and love of Jesus Christ.

When you fail to recognize and understand that God loves you unconditionally, you will never discover your purpose because you will often try to find love and validation in everything and everyone else but God. These people and things will often disappoint you and lead you to a path of lies and destruction.

As a result, you will never fulfill your destiny because you were looking to find your significance in people and inanimate objects. And instead of receiving love from the God of the universe, who loves you and created you for His glory and His specific purpose, you will keep searching for love in the wrong places.

Why and when do women tend to make this mistake?

Women tend to make this mistake because of broken relationships with other people, especially other men. They've allowed people, who don't understand God's love

23

to define them so much that they believe they are not worthy of God's love.

Women often feel unworthy because of all the bad things they've either done or experienced in their lives. As a result, they don't recognize, receive, or embrace God's unconditional love for them.

It's important to understand that no matter what you have done or the mistakes you have made, that God forever loves you, forever values you, forever pursues you, and has forgiven you for everything past, present, and future (Romans 8:1, 39).

The truth is that none of us is worthy of God's love. He loves us because He wants to. All we need to do is to receive it. But what women often fail to realize is that this is why Christ came: for all the sin we've committed and will ever commit – past, present, and future.

Many people, including Christians, have a limited understanding of God's Word. Many don't have a revelation of God's Word for their lives or specific situation. And unless they have a strong relationship with

God, they won't be aware of or fully appreciate God's unconditional love for them.

For instance, like us, you may have grown up in the church. However, even as regular churchgoers, we never understood or embraced the relevance of God's Word in our lives, including His love.

Maybe it was taught, and it just didn't click for you, like it didn't click for us. We just didn't understand because we were lost.

People often make this mistake because they are limited due to the human love that comes with certain conditions and/or strings attached. They can't comprehend God's love because it's never been modeled or demonstrated to them, or they never recognized it when it was show to them.

Since these broken relationships leave women feeling unloved and insecure, they also fail to recognize when God is at work in their lives. The sad thing is that God constantly offers them the unconditional love they so desperately need, but they don't realize this.

People tend to make this mistake when they're focused on achieving their goals on their own terms, apart from God.

It also occurs when they don't believe that God cares for them. And they don't think they are worth God taking the time to love them. People often recognize that God exists, but they don't know Him in a personal way because they don't have a relationship with Him.

They also make this mistake when they feel unloved by the people in their lives and when they feel like they have failed so badly they can't forgive themselves. Or they feel God can't forgive them, and even if He could, why would He?

But God can and will forgive you, and He will if you will receive His forgiveness.

Let me tell you a quick story to illustrate this point...

I (Tiffany) am a church girl.

I've been in the church all of my life, but for many years, I never understood the love of God.

For me, it wasn't "daddy issues." To this day I love my dad and his love for me was often a reflection of God's love. But now that I look at it, I took my dad's love for granted. When I started hearing about people who never had a father in their lives, I understood how precious my father's love was to me. Now I can better appreciate the love my dad shows to me.

When I came to God, I never thought He really cared about the intricate details of my life, the "little things" that were happening, like boyfriend problems, schoolwork, and my personal feelings.

I knew God was real, but I thought He only stepped in when the big problems came.

I really didn't think God cared about me as an individual person, either.

I always looked at God as a distant Being who cared, but not enough to connect with me on a personal basis. For this reason, it was hard for me to talk to God about the personal details of my life. I often felt embarrassed coming into His presence, and I never really wanted to spend intimate time with Him because we weren't that "tight."

This occurred even after I became a Christian. I understood God more when I realized Jesus died for my sins, but I never thought I could carry on a loving, thriving relationship with Him, like I could with a human being.

Eventually I spent time studying strictly on the love of God. I did this for about 1 ½ years until I became more secure in God's love for me.

What Questions Should You Consider?

Questions to consider…

- Why would God love me?

- Does God really love me?

- If so, how do I know for sure? Where's the proof?

- How has God shown His love for me in the past?

- What have people said to me about God in the past to make me doubt His love for me?

- What truths from Scripture can counteract the lies that were said to and about me in the past, as well as God's unconditional love for me?

* Does God really want to experience a personal, intimate relationship with me?

What should you do if you've already made this mistake? How do you fix it?

If you've already fallen into this trap, here's how you get out.

It's important to pull away from everything and everyone during certain seasons, and then ask God Himself to demonstrate His love for you. I did this for weeks and bit by bit, God showed me how much He loved me.

It was somewhat became a "dare" on my part to see how much God really loved me, but God followed through.

For example, one day, on my way inside my church, I read a sign that said, "God loves you!"

Maybe that message had been up for awhile, but God made this real to me on that specific day! And it helped me to believe more that He loved me.

I encourage you to saturate yourself with Scripture and Biblically-based books and messages on God's love. You may want to step away from TV and some of your friends for a while so you can fully concentrate on this topic of God's love.

Now that I am totally convinced of God's love for me, no human being or circumstance can tell me differently. I know God loves me no matter what, and even when I don't feel loved by Him, or even when I feel unlovable, my faith says otherwise.

Say to yourself on a daily basis, "God loves me."

Over time, this one act done on a consistent basis can erase the negative messages and lies that have been poured into you over the years about God's love (or lack of it).

How do we prevent making this mistake moving forward?

Let go of the negative words that others have said to and about you. Then let go of the negative and untrue words[t6] you have said or thought about yourself, no matter how hurtful these words have been. Don't look at yourself, but rather learn to view yourself as God sees you.

Read the Scripture Jeremiah 31:3, memorize and meditate on (ponder) it. Think about it and say it to yourself consistently.

Ask God to show you the different ways He loves you on a daily basis. Recognize the things [t7]and people He uses to demonstrate His love for you, and then thank and praise God for His love for you.

Action Steps for This Chapter

If you want to basically make this a non-issue, here's what you do:

- Get a strong understanding of God's Word. Consider the people in the Bible with whom God had a relationship and loved immensely despite their mistakes. Examples include David, Joseph, Ruth, Mary Magdalene, Rahab, and Paul, to name a few.

- Consistently write down in your journal and recite the statement, "God loves me," until it becomes real to you.

- Write down in your journal the ways God shows you His love.

Books that really helped me to understand God's love include:

- Joyce Meyer's ***Tell Them That I Love Them***

- ***The Love Languages of God*** by Gary Chapman

- ***Reduce Me to Love*** by Joyce Meyer

Our BIGGEST piece of advice moving forward...

Here is my biggest and best piece of advice for you in this area now and moving forward...

In order to receive God's love, you will need to replace the thoughts and messages that constantly tell you God doesn't love you. Replace them with the right messages.

God does love you and nothing can or will change this!

Summary:

Let's summarize:

- Not understanding God's love often comes from broken relationships and negative words spoken to or about you.

- People often fail to recognize and receive God's love when they are preoccupied with their own accomplishments.

- Sometimes it's hard to recognize God's love because we often don't believe He would love us after all the bad things we have done.

- In order to understand and recognize God's love, you will need to replace those messages with God's truth from Scripture and Biblically-based resources.

- Ask God to demonstrate His love for you on a daily basis.

Now that we've covered how to avoid not recognizing God's unconditional love for you, it's time to move on to the NEXT mistake.

MISTAKE #3: IT'S TOO DARK IN HERE!

"...he hath sent me to heal the brokenhearted, to preach deliverance to the captives..." Luke 4:18 (KJV)

What is the mistake?

When you refuse to deal with the hurtful, painful issues, from your past or present

Simply stated, this mistake is...

It's when you're afraid to walk down the dark places in your life. You may ask, "What are **dark places**?"

Dark places are the "scandals" from your past or present that you're ashamed of, but don't want to deal with or address. It's the sin you've committed or what someone did to or against you. It could also be the baggage that you're carrying from previous relationships. All of these things can shape your perception and decision making.

35

Some examples of dark places include:

- Abortion
- Experiencing Molestation/Rape
- Molesting someone else
- Losing your virginity/having sex prior to marriage
- Lesbianism
- Living with someone before marriage
- Anger
- An affair with a married man
- Cutting yourself
- Suicide attempts
- Being promiscuous
- Overeating
- Anorexia/Bulimia
- Greed
- Jealousy
- Abandonment
- Bitterness/Resentment
- Manipulation
- Prostitution
- Being a Stripper

- Incest
- A failed marriage/relationship
- Bankruptcy
- Foreclosure
- Car Repossession
- Jail time
- Pornography addiction
- Daddy issues

If your dark place isn't in the previous list, you can fill in the blank. _____

Dark places also include the hurtful places of your past. Rather than dealing with these dark places, people often act as if their dark places don't even exist, although it affects them in their daily lives.

It's very important to admit that you have dark places.

Instead, many women try to mask the pain. They avoid dealing with the effects of it by replacing their dark places with something or someone else.

And at times, they take their frustration out on those closest to them although these people don't deserve the results of their misdirected emotions.

Why is it a mistake?

This is a mistake because...

Women often don't want to deal with the emotional pain associated with their past. It's too stressful, and it can bring you to a place of frustration or even depression. It can leave you feeling weak, helpless, and powerless. It causes you to feel vulnerable.

Walking through these dark places can reopen the wounds of past hurts and pains you'd prefer to avoid.

Women avoid these dark places by replacing them with awards, degrees, relationships, and other accolades, in hopes that these dark places will go away without them having to deal with the pain. Sometimes women even try to bury their dark places, but unfortunately, when you refuse to deal with these dark places, they will keep resurfacing in various relationships and/or situations.

Often, people continue to make bad choices because they never dealt with the unhealthy patterns they created as a result of their hurtful past.

It's also a mistake to blame others, (who did not contribute to your dark places) as a result of your dark places because the people around you don't deserve to be mistreated and beat down because of what someone else did to you.

For example, our family, friends, boyfriend, or husband could become frustrated with your fighting and angry outbursts. And as a result, they may distance themselves from you, and you could miss out on some rich relationships that could have helped you in your healing process.

What are the consequences of making this mistake and how critical are they?

The consequences of making this mistake are relatively critical because...

When you are afraid to deal with the dark places of your past, you can miss out on God's healing power. God really wants to heal you, but if you don't allow Him to, you will remain hurt and connected to your past because you never addressed it.

In order to overcome your problems, you must face them head on.

When you avoid your past by replacing the healing process with things and people, you may have a limited amount of success in certain areas. However, you will still struggle with the nagging feeling of your past or current sins.

And eventually, no matter what you achieve, you will still feel that emptiness because of the hurt you feel that can only be healed by the power and presence of Jesus Christ. He came to set the captives free, but in order for Him to do this, you must let Him.

Why and when do people tend to make this mistake?

People tend to make these mistakes when they don't think they've been adversely affected by their past although they really have. They make this mistake because they believe that their accomplishments and new relationships will erase the pain they're facing.

They believe that if they can take their frustration out on somebody else, then they are getting revenge for the hurt they endured.

Women tend to make this mistake because the hurt they carry makes them feel like a failure. It often reminds them of a time when they were either a victim or involved in their worst moments of sin.

However, when they have some type of achievement in their lives, they believe this will bring them the healing they are looking for, or at least fill a void they have.

Let me tell you a quick story to illustrate this point...

I had a string of horrible relationships with guys during my teenage years.

As a result, these broken relationships left me feeling used, neglected, angry and rejected.

There was one relationship in particular that had a major impact on me and left me totally resentful of men, and unwilling to properly open my heart to others.

I blamed that one person for everything I had gone through.

For this reason, I eventually took my frustration out on my husband, Dexter on a consistent basis which was unfair to him and our relationship.

For a season, I went on a fast and the Lord showed me that it wasn't just that one person, but my hurt came from a series of relationships where I trusted men, but they often violated my trust.

The road back to normalcy and healing was a long road, but as I allowed God to pull back the layers of my life, He began to heal me. And I began to see God in a new way and appreciate His love for me.

What Questions Should You Consider?

Questions to Consider…

- Why don't I want to deal with my past?
- What were some of the hurtful things from my past?
- How did they make me feel?
- Have they guided my decision-making process?

- Have I allowed my past to hinder me from God's best in certain areas of my life?
- What can I do now to deal with my past?
- What or who do I keep turning to in order to mask the hurt from my past? Why?
- Am I willing to make the sacrifices necessary to overcome my past especially, if it means I can walk in freedom for the rest of my life?

What should you do if you've already made this mistake? How do you fix it?

If you've already fallen into this trap, here's how you get out.

Recognize and admit that you are hurting.

Don't try to hide or deny your dark places from your past (or present) because doing this won't make it go away.

Make a decision to face your dark places head on even if it causes you pain. It's almost like sitting in a well-lit room where you're always used to that type of lighting. Then someone unexpectedly turns the lights off.

You're scared of the dark, and because of this, you don't know how to navigate in the dark. As a result, you run to another room. The rooms represent the other things, people, and accomplishments you run to for safety instead of dealing with the dark places of your life.

There's some good news about walking through your dark places.

Consider that when you break through your dark places, however, this may become your area of ministry where you help others to come out of their dark places. So when you get set free, you can share the love of God to others and give them suggestions for becoming free from the same things you struggled with as well.

How do we prevent making this mistake moving forward?

Before you're hit with the temptation to walk away from your past without dealing with it, encourage yourself. Remember that there is no condemnation, (Romans 8:1). Since you are in Christ Jesus, you are no longer defined by your sin or your pain.

Take some time alone. Take a season to just "do you." Pull away from some relationships, TV, and extra activities. (Note: If you are married, you cannot just walk away from your husband. You may want to ask him to give you some time to spend with God, but you cannot separate from him just to spend time with God 24/7!)

Just use this alone time to spend with God so you can get to the root of your issues.

If the people you spend time with are very close to you, you can talk to them about your past, if you feel comfortable doing this. Make sure they are trustworthy people. But make sure the people you choose to talk to won't throw your past back in your face at a later time or during a moment of anger.

Since my husband often faced the brunt of my emotional outbursts, I shared with him how I felt. (I actually told him about my past before we got married, but what I didn't realize was that I still struggled with the emotional consequences of my sins and issues.)

Action Steps for This Chapter

Based on my experience, here's some insight that can really help you with this issue...

The number one tool I recommend is reading, studying, and meditating on the Word of God. It will help you to heal in places that only God can heal.

You should find Scriptures that relate to your problem(s). Then write them down and memorize them.

Recognize that God has forgiven you, so now you'll need to forgive yourself.

One of the biggest problems I had in overcoming my past relationships was forgiving myself for having premarital sex as a teenager and allowing myself to go so far in my relationships with men.

But once I realized that God had forgiven me, and I could forgive myself, then a heavy load was lifted from me.

Constantly remind yourself that you are God's child and that you are defined by Him, not by what you did in your past.

Our BIGGEST piece of advice moving forward...

Here is my biggest and best piece of advice for you in this area now and moving forward...

Deal with your issues or your issues will deal with you!

In other words, if you don't take time to deal with the dark places of your current sin, past sins, hurts, or other baggage, these dark places will come back to haunt you, and it could destroy your reputation, your good relationships, and the destiny God has for you!

Summary:

Let's summarize:

- Women are often afraid to walk down the dark places of their lives.

- They tend to cover their hurts through accomplishments, education, relationships, and other accolades.

- Recognize and admit that you are hurting.

- Because of a hurtful past, we often feel a need to get revenge. And we often take that revenge out on those closest to us.

- Remember that God has forgiven you so you should forgive yourself.

- Now that we've gotten past the CURRENT MISTAKE, it's time to go over how to avoid the NEXT MISTAKE.

MISTAKE #4: I'M TOO BUSY FOR THAT!

"Your word _is_ a lamp to my feet And a light to my path." Psalm 119:15

What is the mistake?

Not taking time to read God's Word and spend quiet time with Him.

It occurs when a person does not make time for God.

The Bible, God's Word is a lamp to our feet and a light to our path. It is the infallible Word of God. And as Christians, we must believe that God's Word works 100% of the time for every situation we face.

However, many Christians, unfortunately, don't believe that the entire Word of God is true. And as a result, they consult friends, family members, co-workers, psychics, horoscopes, and other often unreliable sources, instead of the Bible.

In addition, many women struggle with spending time in God's presence. They don't value the precious moments that God offers His children. This is unfortunate because spending quiet time in God's presence is one of the main ways to build a relationship with Him.

What does it mean to spend time in God's presence?

Just like any other person who loves you, God is a Person who wants you to spend time with Him. It occurs when you make room for God to feel at home in your heart. It begins with a desire to seek God with a sincere heart.

Spending time in God's presence can involve quiet time, singing, praise, journaling, and any other way you can enjoy time with Him. God really cares for you, and when you make time to spend in His presence, it pleases Him.

Being quiet and still is a great way to seek God. It enables you to clear your mind so you can prepare your heart to receive and hear from Him.

There are so many benefits to spending time with God.

For one, being in God's presence enables you to connect with Him on an intimate level through your prayer, declaration of His Word, thanksgiving, studying God's Word, singing, etc. It helps you to step outside of yourself and your circumstances and into a world filled with His love and presence.

However, when you don't spend time in God's Word or His presence, it becomes difficult to apply His Word in a practical way on a daily basis. Then when tough times hit, instead of relying on the Word of God to guide you, it becomes more tempting to call your friends, complain, try to solve the problems yourself, or even wait until the situation becomes uncontrollable and chaotic before going to God.

Why is it a mistake?

This is a mistake because...

When you don't study God's Word, you won't recognize when God speaks. You will hear a lot of voices, and you will not be able to discern between God's voice, your voice, other people's opinions, and even Satan's voice.

And then what makes sense or seems logical to you may not be God's plan. But you'll look for guidance and come up with a "bright" idea, for instance. It may be a plan you "concocted" because it felt good to your flesh instead something you received from the Holy Spirit.

God tells us that His ways are not our ways and His plans are higher than ours, (Isaiah 55:8-9). However, if we can't recognize God's voice, we will find ourselves doing a lot of stuff, but remaining stuck and stagnate in our walk with Him.

Also, when you don't spend time in God's presence, you will often make bad decisions. This becomes a pattern in your life, and these decisions can lead you down a destructive path, (Proverbs 16:25.)

When you don't apply God's Word, you will apply your own experiences or opinions to your situation. This can become dangerous, and when you continue to do this, you will deceive yourself.

What are the consequences of making this mistake and how critical are they?

The consequences of making this mistake are extremely critical because...

When you don't use God's Word as your standard and ultimate guide, you could make a series of bad decisions. As a result, you will weave yourself into a web of frustration and broken dreams because you failed to get insight from God.

When you don't spend time in God's presence, you will be left with a void, and you will find someone or something else to fill this void.

For example, consider your friends and acquaintances with whom you spend time.

Unless your friends or acquaintances are people you connect with are stable and godly, they could ultimately destroy you. If their advice sounds good to you or validates your opinion(s), you will continue to follow these individuals, even when they go against the Word of God.

Ultimately, it will lead you farther away from God's destiny and purpose for your life.

Also not using God's Word can open you up to confusion and deception. Even when you want to hear from God, it will come only in spurts because you don't have the ever-flowing influence of God's Word to direct you.

As a result, you could compromise your mind and heart by consulting ungodly people, TV shows, and circumstances to direct you.

You could learn how to override the Holy Spirit's promptings because when God actually does speak to you, it will sound foreign and it will go contrary to your "normal" way of thinking. It just won't make sense because you haven't spent time in God's Word to find the truth about your situation(s).

Why and when do people tend to make this mistake?

People tend to make this mistake when they have not been taught how important the Word of God is to their lives.

Instead of seeking God, people also make this mistake when they allow distractions such as TV, movies, social media, and other activities take the place of their personal Bible Study and worship.

It's not to say that TV, social media, movies, etc. are bad. But everything you do must be done in moderation.

Many people did not grow up in the church, so they don't recognize the value of God's Word. Nor do they recognize spending time in His presence. And others who grew up in the church may know God, but never learned to how to prioritize His Word or how to spend time with Him.

Also, many people believe that the Pastor or Bible teacher is totally responsible for giving them the Word of God. However, we must do personal Bible Study so the Holy Spirit can speak to us on a personal, consistent basis.

Unfortunately, many people believe they have tried to study the Bible, but they often read a version of the Bible that is too difficult and become frustrated, so they give up.

Instead, they look to other written and digital sources, and maybe other religions and philosophies that seem easier to understand. They think these things will help them as they try to find answers to their problems.

People struggle with spending time in God's presence because they don't make time to be still in order to hear His voice. Often God speaks to us in a still small voice. But if we don't make time to be still, we will not hear His voice when He does speak because we haven't taken the time to connect with Him.

God speaks to us in various ways:

- His written Word (the Bible)
- His preached Word
- The Holy Spirit
- People
- Circumstances
- Dreams and Visions
- Visions
- Peace
- Counsel

Many people weren't taught the practicality of God's Word, so they don't think it's relevant for this time or for their lives. They often seek out the words and wisdom of the latest "guru," celebrity, political figure, psychic, or Christian leader as their authority. But they don't look at the timeless Word of God as their guide.

When a person searches and they find another type of book or person who can tell them what they want to hear, they will gravitate to these sources. They seek out new fads and trends that will validate their feelings, actions, and the decisions they've already made. This is not the best route because many people, books, and fads change from day to day, and are often unreliable and false.

Let me tell you a quick story to illustrate this point...

I have been saved for over 20 years. But it was only about 10 years ago that I started using God's Word as the ultimate guide for my life. Yes, I was saved, and I knew I was going to heaven. And I could even quote Bible verses at the right time.

But I often made decisions based on logic and experience instead of the Word of God. Then when life's tests came, I often found myself frustrated with myself, God, and those around me.

I would become angry with myself because I often felt stuck. I was angry with God because I knew He could change the situation immediately, but refused to do so. I blamed Him for getting me into the messes I was in.

Because after all, if He was God and He could do anything, why couldn't He deliver me from my problems?

Because of my frustrating circumstances, I often believed that God didn't love me. I thought if I could just praise Him a little more or if I could get involved in more ministries at church, then He would answer my prayers and bless me.

Not to mention, my prayers were often focused on God rescuing me from my current situations. I often felt lonely, frustrated, and bewildered because I couldn't understand why God wasn't blessing me or giving me what I needed, wanted, or felt I deserved from Him.

But eventually, I had a series of life changes.

I went on a "love journey" with God. I began to study the love of God and I realized that God's love wasn't based on my circumstances. In fact, I realized that God loved me unconditionally and He really did care about me.

Also, I now realize that God cares for me in the "minor" and "major" areas of my life.

What questions should you consider?

Questions to Consider...

- Who do I believe God is?

- Do I believe God loves me unconditionally?

- Do I believe He cares about every aspect of my life, including the "little" things?

- Do I believe that God's Word can lead me in making proper life decisions?

- Do I really believe that I can experience joy in God's presence?

- What things do I allow to keep me distracted from studying God's Word?

- What can I let go of in order to study God's Word more often and more effectively?

- Is there a version of the Bible that I can understand better?

What should you do if you've already made this mistake? How do you fix it?

If you've already fallen into this trap, here's how you get out.

Confess: Tell God you are sorry for not spending time in His Word.

Repent or change your mind about your perspective on Him. Remember that God loves you unconditionally, (no matter what you have done or where you are in your life.) He also has a specific plan for your life.

Recognize that since God is the ultimate Planner, He has a blueprint for your life which can only be found by seeking Him through His Word and spending personal time with Him.

Take 5 minutes to sit in complete silence, so you can practice being still to hear God's voice. Do this on a daily basis. Add 5 minutes to your quiet time each week, if possible.

Pray and ask God for guidance and direction. Ask Him for clarity and wisdom.

As you sit quietly, think about God's goodness and meditate (which means to think, consider, or ponder) about a specific Bible verse that has been on your heart. Try to picture this verse in your mind.

Begin to journal what you believe God spoke to you during your moments of silence. Write down any questions or concerns you may have as well.

How do we prevent making this mistake moving forward?

Here's what you should do to prevent this mistake from happening moving forward...

Make up in your mind that God's Word is 100% true and it is relevant to you for every area in your life.

Spend quiet time thinking, meditating on God's Word, and doing whatever it takes to hear from Him.

Make sure you consistently attend a local church that is loving, teaches the Word of God, and believes it's true.

Most likely what you've been learning with God all week will be confirmed during the preaching and worship, if you have an open heart to receive what God is saying.

Action Steps for This Chapter

Here's a way you can get even better results by doing things a bit differently...

For many people, reading the Bible can be a challenging task.

This is why it's good to approach Bible reading in small steps. Pray and ask God to lead you and make His word understandable to you. When you do this, consider the version of Bible you want to use.

Many people often own a King James Version, (KJV) of the Bible laying around the house somewhere. But they often complain that it's too difficult to read.

There are other versions of the Bible that are a little more contemporary and easier to read without taking away from the meaning of Scripture.

Some of these versions include:

- New King James Version (NKJV)
- New International Version (NIV)
- Message (MSG)
- New American Standard Bible (NASB)

I recommend you start by reading one of the Gospels, (Matthew, Mark, Luke, or John). Or you could start with the book of Psalms or Proverbs. Write down some keywords that stick out in your mind.

You can do this by answering some of the following questions:

- What was the overall mood of the Scripture?
- Who wrote the book?
- Who was it written to?
- When was it written?
- Why was it written?
- What was the writer saying in this passage of Scripture?
- What does this passage of Scripture mean to you?

Also, you can purchase a good, reliable study Bible. A good one that has helped me over the years is called the

Life Application Bible. It's filled with great information on Scripture, including commentaries on specific verses, profiles on Biblical figures, and other historical facts. This will give you a good context of Scripture so you will know how to properly apply the right Scriptures to your situation.

I recommend you purchase the book, workbook, and DVD set called *4 Keys to Hearing God's Voice*. This book changed my life. It offers a proven, Biblically based system for learning to hear the voice of God clearly.

I learned that I could hear God's voice by doing four things:

- Being still/quiet to hear God's voice.
- Fixing my eyes on Jesus.
- Spontaneous thoughts that could ultimately come from God.
- Journaling what I feel God is saying to me.

Since learning these tips, my life has changed, and I have learned to hear God's voice on a more consistent basis. The great thing is that I enjoy being in God's presence because I expect to hear Him say something to me on a daily basis.

Make a decision to spend at least 5-10 minutes a day in God's presence by being quiet and then journaling about what you hear Him say. Recognize that it's okay to make mistakes as you learn to hear God's voice. Doing this often takes some time to learn, so don't beat yourself up because you don't get to hear God clearly the first few times. It often requires practice.

It's important to know what God says based on His Word, and not our emotions, feelings, friends, or circumstances. Each one of these has a voice that competes for our attention.

Which voice will you listen to?

In addition to spending quiet time with God, we recommend that you ask God to lead you to a good friend or mentor who truly knows the Word of God. Make sure this person is sincere, and their life reflects the principles of God's Word.

The person you confide in about time with God and journaling should be able to recognize the voice of God in their own lives. They should also be going in a positive direction and have a level of success to prove that reading, internalizing, and applying God's Word works.

Our BIGGEST piece of advice moving forward...

Make time to read God's Word every day. And even if you don't "feel" anything, read it because God often works in process. In other words, while you may not see an outward change, He often makes changes on the inside of us before we see the outward results. And while we're reading God's word, we're getting to know Him better, and we are growing in our faith.

Summary:

Let's summarize:

* It's important to make time to study God's Word.

* People tend to make the mistake of not reading the Bible when they have not been taught on the importance of God's Word to their lives.

* They often replace God's Word with TV, other people, or activities

- One reason why people struggle to get in the presence of God is because they often find it difficult to become still.

- The way to hear God's voice is to be still, fix your eyes on Christ, spontaneous thoughts, and journaling.

- Ask God to lead you to a good friend/mentor who knows, applies, and understands the Bible well, and who can lovingly show you how to walk out your life as a Christian.

Now that we've covered how to avoid the CURRENT MISTAKE, it's time to move on to the NEXT MISTAKE.

MISTAKE #5: OUCH, THAT HURT!

"Then He said to the disciples, "It is impossible that no offenses should come, but woe *to him* through whom they do come!" Luke 17:1

What is the mistake?

Refusing to forgive or get over an offense.

This occurs when people become offended and refuse to forgive people, institutions, systems, or experiences that hurt, violated, or disappointed them. It also includes not forgiving yourself.

In other words, when you refuse to let a bad situation go.

Why is it a mistake?

This is a mistake because unforgiveness blocks you from hearing God's voice clearly and experiencing His blessings.

It's also a mistake because when you don't forgive yourself or others, you hinder your growth and purpose because you continue to see things from a negative and improper perspective.

Lastly, it's a mistake because forgiveness is the gift you give yourself. However, when you don't forgive, you rob yourself of the abundant life that God promises His children.

What are the consequences of making this mistake and how critical are they?

The consequences of making this mistake are extremely critical which means...

When you don't forgive others, you will continue to make bad decisions from the filter of your anger, resentment, and unforgiveness. You will make people who remind you of the person(s) who hurt you, suffer because you never forgave them.

For instance, if your father was never in your life, then you may have an issue of trust or respect when it comes to men in general. As a result, you could find yourself becoming negative or hostile to your male boss, boyfriend, or husband because of what your father did to you.

When don't let go of a system, experience, or situation, you'll allow fear or anger to hinder you from the very place God could be calling you to go. This was the case with Naomi, the mother-in-law of Ruth.

Naomi became bitter due to the loss of her husband and sons, (Ruth 1:20.) But eventually Naomi learned to let go of her hurt and pain. As a result, she influenced Ruth who left a legacy and was part of the lineage that led to David and ultimately our Savior Jesus Christ, (Matthew 1:5-18.)

Why and when do women tend to make this mistake?

People often make the mistake of not forgiving when they have not forgiven themselves.

They tend not to forgive themselves because they may still feel guilty for what they have done. They fail to recognize that God's forgiveness is more powerful than their own forgiveness. And they unnecessarily beat themselves up.

I, (Tiffany), struggled with unforgiveness for a long time until I discovered God's unconditional love for me. I realized that God's love covered my sin, so I should let it go as well.

And I also realized that holding onto unforgiveness and not letting it go was a trick of the enemy. He wanted to keep me distracted and wrapped up in my own guilt and self-loathing.

How can you be effective for God if you consider yourself the scum of the earth?

It's impossible!

People tend to make this mistake when they...

For one, they find it hard to forgive when they feel violated or betrayed by someone. And they also struggle with unforgiveness when they have put unrealistic expectations on someone only to have the person fail at meeting their expectations. Then when their expectations go unmet, they feel disappointed by the person. And the person is now on their "bad side" or "hit list."

People also make this mistake when they have had one or more bad experiences, and they associate that one bad experience with everything else they face, even the new ones.

For instance, let's say you traveled to New York for vacation and got mugged. While this is very tragic, you shouldn't avoid going to New York or travelling again, just because of that one bad experience. Just put your money in a different place or go with a group of people next time.

Don't rob yourself of enjoying the rich, cultural experience of a big city like New York because of that one situation! The same goes with relationships, situations and systems.

Try again. Just make some adjustments.

People tend not to forgive themselves when they believe that their sin is too bad to forgive, or when they are still suffering as a result of their sin. For example, if a woman has had a baby out of wedlock, and doesn't forgive herself, she will constantly beat herself up because she has to deal with that child everyday. While pre-marital sex is a sin all life comes from God. Regardless of how the child was conceived, God still loves that mother and her child…and even the baby's daddy!

Let me tell you a quick story to illustrate this point...

A lot of people have been hurt in the church, but I never understood church hurt until I experienced it for myself.

I, (Tiffany) grew up in the church, but it wasn't until I was 20 years old that I had an understanding of Christ and accepted Him as my personal Savior.

God became real to me, and my new found faith was exciting. I shared Jesus with everyone I met. And I loved my new church. I had become very active at this church. And this was the church where I met and married my husband.

However, after about seven years at this church, things started changing.

A lot of decisions were made that I did not agree with, and some of the people who I revered and respected became very hurtful towards me. Because of this, I became confused. I didn't understand how Christian leadership could be so hurtful.

In addition, I battled with some of the issues from my past that were unrelated to church, so I dealt with a lot. However, I now realize that God was using these situations to bring me into a deeper relationship with Him.

For various reasons, we left this church a couple years later. I left the church feeling, confused, rejected, and angry. Since I was very active at this church, I felt that God could never use me again. And I refused to trust leadership at any church.

In fact, I had made a decision never to join a church again, but instead, visit different churches on a weekly basis.

But one Sunday morning about two years after leaving our last church, I heard a message called, "Stick and Stay." The minister spoke about the importance of getting rooted at a church and staying committed, not to man, but to God. And as a result, I would reap God's blessings.

During that sermon, God changed my heart about church and church leadership. My heart still needed to be healed, but eventually, my husband and I finally joined another church, and I have learned to forgive those who hurt me. It wasn't easy, but I went through the process of healing and forgiveness.

What Questions Should You Consider?

Questions to consider...

- Have you ever been hurt by something or someone?
- Was it a one-time event or was it a constant issue?
- Were you violated by someone or did someone fail to meet your expectations?
- Did you put unrealistic expectations on someone? If so, why?
- Was it realistic for this person to meet these expectations?
- Have you done something that you're ashamed to admit you did?
- Why can't you forgive yourself?
- Are you avoiding something or someone new because of a previous bad experience that went wrong?

- Do you realize that you could be hindering or cutting off your blessings because you refuse to forgive?
- Is there anything too hard for God to forgive?

We can answer this question. No! This means that you also can forgive others…and yourself!

What should you do if you've already made this mistake? How do you fix it?

If you've already fallen into this trap, here's how you get out.

Admit to God and yourself what happened to hurt you. He's the best person to talk to. He wants to hear from you, and He wants you to be honest about how you feel.

At times it can be tempting to tell your friends when someone else hurt you, but if this person can't give you godly advice and direction, it's probably not the best option to talk with them. This could only anger you more, and it could cause the other person to have unnecessary ill-feelings towards the person who hurt you.

Recognize that you can't forgive on your own. Often you will need time, and you will definitely need the presence of the Holy Spirit to heal your heart from this hurt.

You will eventually need to trust God to help you let it go if you want to pursue your God-given purpose. This is not as easy for some as it is for others depending, on your personality and the severity of your hurt. It took me many years to let go of my church hurt, but my hope is that if I am ever hurt in this way again, I can forgive and let it go much more quickly.

Remember that forgiveness frees you to become all that God has called you to be. And forgiveness is the gift you give yourself.

How do we prevent making this mistake moving forward?

Here's what you should do to prevent this mistake from happening moving forward...

Don't ever put your trust solely in one person.

Also refuse to put all of your expectations in people because humans, (including us), are flaky, and short-sighted. While you may have certain goals and expectations, others may not have the same as yours.

There's nothing wrong with putting expectations on people especially if they say they will fulfill them, but don't be surprised if they fall through or don't do them at all.

Pray and ask God to direct you in your expectations. When you trust God first, He will prepare you for whatever outcome occurs.

For example, a lot of people tend to exclude God from their lives when it comes to pursuing their relationships. But then when the relationship(s) fail, they blame God when it doesn't work.

When you focus on God, He will keep you grounded in your expectations of other people and systems. He will often enable you to discern the motives of other people before you get too close in your relationship with them.

The key is for you to take note of the "red flags." The red flags are obvious signs that give you the uncomfortable

HELP, I'M STUCK!

feelings you experience when something doesn't feel, look, sound, or seem right to you.

Don't let a few bad experiences stop you from trying something again, especially if God is calling you back into that area. For instance, let's say you're a track runner and you run the 200 meter dash. If you come in 4th place each time, don't drop out of track totally. You may need to train harder.

Or you may need to try another track event such as the 400 meter dash or the long jump, but don't just give up on track altogether unless God tells you to give up!

Action Steps for This Chapter

Based on my experience, here's some insight that can really help you with this issue...

Understand that God wants you to walk in forgiveness on a consistent basis. For this reason, I would definitely recommend having a long talk with God. This may take more than one time of prayer.

Just begin to rest in God's presence. Renew your fellowship with Him. Regardless of who left you or who you left, God is always there waiting to spend time with you. Take this time to vent, shout, scream, and get everything out. He can take it and He also cares, (1 Peter 5:7).

Ask God to help you for the next steps you need to take in the process of forgiveness. Also, being **in God's presence** will heal things that other things can't.

Begin to think about any part you played in the catastrophe(s) you experienced.

Note, if you were violated and endured a traumatic situation, such as molestation or rape, this was definitely not your fault!

But you do need to recognize that you will eventually need to forgive the person who violated you.

Also, recognize that the person(s) who hurt or violated you may never apologize for what they did to you. So don't try to get justice from them. God will vindicate you for the pain you faced, although it may not be the way you want or expect, (Romans 12:19).

In addition, God will heal you from your hurts. But if you keep trying to get your offender to repay you for what they did to you, you may waste a lot of precious time.

I must admit, it took me many years to forgive people who hurt me, from my bullies in elementary school, to those who lied on me in middle school, and to the adults who either violated or disrespected me. I spent a lot of time angry and bitter with these people.

I also realized something, I was holding onto the unforgiveness of a memory. In most cases, the people who hurt me no longer had the power to do it anymore…unless I chose to hold onto the pain of that memory.

Also, I later realized that my offenders were not trying to hurt me as much as they were trying to fulfill their selfish needs and desires.

Also, forgiveness does not mean that I needed to be best friends with those who hurt me. Nor did it mean that the relationship would ever be mended.

The key was for me to forgive and let go regardless of how that person felt about me or regardless of whether they ever apologized or not.

To begin your forgiveness journey, I recommend you start with the Bible. I would recommend finding at least one or two Scriptures on forgiveness that speak to your heart. Begin to memorize and meditate on them. This way, when the temptation to become angry comes up, you can fight it with the Word of God.

I would also suggest that you seek healing. Anytime you've been hurt, violated, or angered, you'll need to be healed. It took me time to get healed from my past and my church hurt. In addition to the Word, I read some books on healing and forgiveness.

Three of the many books I recommend include:

Beauty for Ashes by Joyce Meyer

The Bait of Satan by John Bevere

Let it Go by TD Jakes.

Pivotal Prayer by John Hull and Tim Elmore

These books helped me to look at forgiveness from an entirely new perspective. It took a lot of time, but I made it. While there are still some areas of forgiveness I still need to work on, I'm a lot better than I was a few years ago.

Be willing to review these materials from time to time because offense can come at any time, from any place.

The question is, how will you respond after it happens the next time?

My BIGGEST piece of advice moving forward...

Here is my biggest and best piece of advice for you in this area now and moving forward...

If you refuse to let go of your unforgiveness, you will live your life in bitterness, resentment, and shame. And the devil will use this to hinder you from pursuing God's best for you. Do your part to forgive and let it go because if you don't God will keep you in a holding place that will leave you frustrated, confused, and unproductive in everything you do.

Summary:

Let's summarize:

- Unforgiveness can occur when you place unrealistic expectations on others or when someone violates you.

- When you refuse to forgive, you will make bad decisions because you filter everything through your unforgiveness and resentment.

- Don't let one or two bad situations cause you to give up or avoid something.

- If you were violated, such as through rape or molestation, this was not your fault. But you will still need to forgive the person who violated you.

- God wants you to become whole and walk in forgiveness.

- He will help you to forgive.

Now that we've gotten past the mistake of unforgiveness, it's time to go over how to avoid the NEXT MISTAKE.

MISTAKE #6: PUSH IT!

"Be strong and of good courage, do not fear nor be afraid of them; for the LORD your God, He *is* the One who goes with you. He will not leave you nor forsake you." Deuteronomy 31:6

What is the mistake?

Allowing fear to hinder you from walking in your purpose

This mistake happens when people allow fear to hinder or paralyze them from doing great things instead of trusting God and walking in courage.

This happens when people pull back from pursuing purpose when opposition attacks. People allow fear to hinder them from becoming all that God has called them to become. They often worry about what people will say to or about them versus what God says about them.

Many people fail to understand that Jesus Christ, their God and Creator is most important. In fact, God's opinion is really the only one that counts, especially when there is a decision to make.

Why is it a mistake?

This is a mistake because pulling back when fear or some other opposition attacks, gives the enemy the chance to gain the victory in your life. And it stops God from getting the glory out of your life.

Fear is an acquired emotion that can control you if you're not careful.

It's also a mistake to operate in fear and become a people pleaser since people's opinions of you can change from day to day. People's opinions are very inconsistent, and they are never good indicators as to whether you are on track with God or not.

While God's methods may change, He remains the same based on His Word.

He says, "For I *am* the LORD, I do not change…" (Malachi 3:6)

What are the consequences of making this mistake and how critical are they?

The consequences are that you will never fulfill your purpose because you let opposition, circumstances, and people dictate your direction in life.

Fear, which is a learned emotion will cause you to miss out on the things you've been praying for as well as the wonderful plans God has for you. As you begin to learn God's Word and spend time with Him, the plan He has for you will become clearer and more realistic to you.

And as a result, you can walk in confidence without allowing fear to stop you from walking in faith.

On the other hand, if you allow people's opinion to dictate your direction in life, you will find yourself confused, frustrated, and unproductive. Ultimately you will become miserable, resentful, and hateful because you listened to man rather than God. And instead, of walking in faith, you will walk in fear.

Why and when do people tend to make this mistake?

People tend to make this mistake because many people don't like to deal with conflict.

Somewhere in their lives they learned to handle and/or avoid situations as a result of fear. For this reason, they tend to view situations through the eyes of fear instead of courage and boldness.

A clear example of this was when the 12 spies went to Canaan to survey the land in Numbers 13:31-33:

"But the men who had gone up with him said, 'We are not able to go up against the people, for they are stronger than we.'

And they gave the children of Israel a bad report of the land which they had spied out, saying, "The land through which we have gone as spies is a land that devours its inhabitants, and all the people whom we saw in it are men of great stature. There we saw the giants[a] (the descendants of Anak came from the giants); and we were like grasshoppers in our own sight, and so we were in their sight."

From the above passage, we see that ten of the men said it was impossible to possess the land because of the people who lived there. And the ten spies saw themselves as grasshoppers, and the giants of the land saw them as grasshoppers as well.

Note: People will see and treat you based on how you see and treat yourself.

We often allow our circumstances and people's opinions to dictate our life decisions because we want to be liked and validated. This is unfortunate because in many cases we can do a lot of things only to find ourselves still disliked by other people.

Women often make this decision when they are not passionate about what they are pursuing. When you're passionate, you learn to develop a "pit bull" mentality, and you fight to win. You pursue your goal(s), regardless of the opposition.

But when you are not passionate or indifferent, you allow people, things, and situations to block you from going after your purpose.

People also make this mistake when they allow the voice of fear to speak louder to them than the voice of God. Often they don't realize that God has an emotional investment in their purpose and other life decisions because they don't recognize how much He loves them. Even in our fear, God's love helps us to overcome it when we choose to trust Him with every step of our lives, (1 John 4:18).

In the story of the twelve spies who went to look at Canaan, only two of the twelve, Joshua and Caleb were tenacious and bold enough to go into the land and possess it.

In Numbers 13:30, Joshua and Caleb were in the minority because they trusted God to help them take possession of the land. Joshua and Caleb were different and stood out from their other ten counterparts, who allowed fear to stop them from doing what God called them to do.

Have you ever feared being in the minority when a decision needed to be made?

How many of us go along with the crowd because we fear believing what God says, and fear being in the minority?

Of course being in the minority can be scary, intimidating, and lonely. But I would rather be with God in the minority than to be against him with the majority, (Romans 8:31).

Let us tell you a quick story to illustrate this point...

When I, (Tiffany) was a little girl, I was often bullied and teased by my peers.

Because of this, I often became overwhelmed with fear and anxiety. And since I wanted to try to fit in, I found myself compromising my values and doing things I normally didn't do, just to fit in.

But the problem was, no matter what I did I never met my peers' approval.

During this time, I was in church, but I didn't have a relationship with Christ. So for this reason, I was not able to get a clear understanding of God's direction and purpose for my life. In fact, I spent a lot of wasted time trying to please people. And ultimately I spent many years in my early adulthood resenting those same people who rejected me as a child.

Eventually, I realized that God used many of these people to reject me so He could protect me.

As a result of not "fitting in," I would eventually come running to Him. These people were inadvertently used by God to push me away from destruction and into His plan for my life. Since gaining this revelation, I have learned to let go and forgive, because I now realize that even as a child God was working in my life ultimately for His glory.

What Questions Should You Consider?

Here's what you should consider…

- What am I pursuing?

- Am I pursuing it with passion?

- What opposition continues to hinder me from pursuing my purpose?

- What event(s) in my life have caused me to operate in fear versus courage?

- Do I really understand the perfect unconditional love that God has for me?

- Do I allow fear to control me?

- Am I a people pleaser?

- Do I consult God first on my decision making?

- Do I find myself asking for the opinions of people?

- Where has this method landed me thus far?

- Do the people I consult have a strong, thriving relationship with Christ?

- Do they have my best interest in mind?

What should you do if you've already made this mistake? How do you fix it?

If you have already made this mistake, identify this opposition and consider the root of it.

Then figure out what this will do to you if you allowed this opposition to stop you from pursuing your destiny.

Begin to replace your fear with courage. The best way to do this is to search Scriptures on fear and overcoming this fear with courage. One Scripture that comes to mind is, "The Lord is my light and my salvation, whom shall I fear?" (Psalm 27:1)

As you meditate and focus on God's Word, start to place your trust in God by seeking Him for advice. While there's nothing wrong with asking friends who are rooted in God's word about some of your decisions, your final answers should ultimately come from God.

Also, you have a mind of your own as well. So when you come to a conclusion, take it to God and see if you have peace about the decision you are about to make.

How do we prevent making this mistake moving forward?

Here's what you should do to prevent this mistake from happening moving forward...

Trust the God in you. The Holy Spirit is your Guide, and He will never lead you astray because He's God. If you struggle with recognizing that God lives in you and He will help you to make decisions, I would suggest spending some time with Him.

Get to learn God's Word and discover His view so that when you make decisions you will have an idea of where He's leading you instead of being completely oblivious about the situation you're in.

Recognize that fear is a trick of the enemy. God has not given you a spirit of fear, but of power, love, and a sound mind, (2 Timothy 1:7). This paralyzing fear you experience is not from God.

Pull away from people for a while and take time to get into the presence of God. Be still and ask God what He wants you to do.

Action Steps for this Chapter

Here's a way you can get even better results by doing things a bit differently...

Begin to write out what your plans are and what you need to do in order to pursue your passion with courage and vigor. Speak Scriptures that are related to your situation. Speak them aloud and apply this Word to your life. Also, submitting to these truths drives the enemy away, (James 4:7).

Another thing I recommend is taking time to assess your friendships. You must be careful who you allow to speak into your life.

Create a list of your friends. Then ask yourself the following questions about each one of your relationships. Be honest with yourself in answering the following questions:

- "Is it worth spending my time with them?"
- "Do they constantly give to me or constantly take from me?"
- "Do I constantly give to them or constantly take from them?"
- "Do they give wise, godly counsel?"
- "Do they confront me in love when I'm wrong or are they overly critical?"

- "Are they a positive or negative force in my life?"
- "Am I stronger and wiser after connecting with them?"
- "Are they pushing me to become God's best or allowing me to settle for mediocrity?"
- "Would I be better or worse if I let them go?"

Once you can honestly answer these questions about each one of your friends, you may be able to let go of some of them more quickly. If there are some friends you are unsure of, then pray about it.

But for the ones who pass your "friend test" praise God for them and cherish them. You may even want to text or call them right now to thank them for being such great friends to you.

My BIGGEST piece of advice moving forward...

Here is my biggest and best piece of advice for you in this area now and moving forward...

Don't allow fear to stop you from doing what God has called you to do because if you do, you will find yourself stuck in a very miserable situation because you held onto fear instead of faith.

Summary:

Let's summarize:

- Fear is a learned emotion.

- People often allow fear to speak louder to them than God. Often they don't realize that God has an emotional investment in their purpose and other life decisions because they don't recognize how much He loves them.

- Begin to place your trust in God by seeking Him for advice. While there's nothing wrong with asking friends who are rooted in God's word about some of your decisions, your final decision should come from God.

- Trust the God in you to help you make a decision.

- Assess your friendships by writing down a list of your friends. Decide on whether or not they are good friends.

- Now that we've gotten past the CURRENT MISTAKE, it's time to go over how to avoid next mistake.

Mistake #7: Girls, Girls, Girls!

"As iron sharpens iron, So a man sharpens the countenance of his friend." Proverbs 27:17

What is the mistake?

Lacking close female friendships due to distrust, insecurity, or hurt.

This happens when women don't have other female friends to connect with in their lives. They don't recognize the value of good, healthy female relationships. It occurs when women can't get along with one another because of past issues due to insecurity and distrust.

This also happens when women don't believe they need each other to help them to pursue their destiny or purpose. They try to do everything on their own because they think that teaming up with other women, to learn new things and get different ideas is a waste of time.

They say things like, "I've got Jesus and that's enough..." or "I have everything I need. Why should I team up with anyone else?"

The reason why you should team up with others is because unity among sisters is a beautiful thing, (Psalm 133:1.) When sisters are connected in a sincere, godly manner, they can encourage one another, and God will get the glory because He dwells in unity and love.

Why is it a mistake?

It's a mistake because women need at least one or two other females with whom they can become transparent.

This is important.

As women, we tend to wrestle with a lot of emotions. Eventually, we must vent to someone through intimate, heartfelt conversation. It can't always be another man she talks with because men don't understand everything women go through.

However, for some reason, we rob ourselves of this opportunity by distancing ourselves from other women.

When women can't get along, it causes a lot of strife and division. And this is how the enemy hinders them from becoming all they can be in Christ. No one person can do everything, despite the "image" women try to protect and maintain.

We don't need to act as if our weaknesses don't exist. Instead, we need to recognize and admit our weaknesses, and then prayerfully find out what other people possess those strengths. Then consider how your strengths can compensate for their weaknesses and vice versa.

A lot of women try to be "Superwoman" by attempting to hide their weaknesses. It's a mistake because as human beings, we have strengths and weaknesses. And we need others because they can offer their strengths in our areas of weakness and vice versa.

In addition, if we never struggled with weaknesses why would we need God?

What are the consequences of making this mistake and how critical are they?

The consequences of making this mistake are critical because...

When women don't have female friends, they can end up lonely and unbalanced because they have no one to become transparent with, other than their male friends, boyfriends, or husbands.

They find themselves sharing their hearts with men, which could cause unnecessary emotional and soul ties with the wrong types of people. Or it could push the good men in their lives away because your man cannot be your girlfriend!

Every woman needs **at least** one or two close female friends with whom she can share her heart and innermost thoughts.

Men, including husbands, are good, but there are some things that only women can understand and relate to about women. This is why it's necessary to have some close female friends.

When women don't get along with each other, it just perpetuates disunity in the Body of Christ and causes them to miss out on what God wants to do in their lives. It also perpetuates the theory that women can't get along, including Christian women!

When women try to "fly solo" they will find themselves incomplete. They will constantly feel like there's a gap in their lives, and the hole that's missing can only be filled by either connecting, partnering, or collaborating with someone through female friendship and interaction.

Why and when do women tend to make this mistake?

Women tend to make this mistake because they often don't trust other women. They have in many cases experienced the pettiness that other women bring to the table.

As a result, many women would rather avoid (what they consider), the drama altogether because they feel it will frustrate, limit, or hinder them from pursuing their purpose.

Also, insecurity can cause women to make this mistake. If a woman feels that she will be "upstaged" or "outshined" by another woman, she may pull back from connecting with her because it may cause her to look less spectacular in the eyes of other people.

They also fear connecting with other women because they fear rejection. They've tried many times to connect with females, only to be snubbed or ignored by them. This can be a hurtful situation to deal with. In fact, this was often the case with me (Tiffany) in various walks of life, both in the spiritual and secular arenas. For this reason, it took me a long time to find and establish good, quality friendships.

Often a woman's hurtful past (with other women), shouts louder than her destiny and she makes the decision not to deal with other women on any level unless it's absolutely necessary. This hurt could come from "mommy" issues, broken friendships, or past betrayals from other women.

Sometimes women become so used to doing things and obtaining success on their own, that they figure, "Why rock the boat? If it's been working for me this long, I don't need anybody now to mess up my 'flow'…"

But if a woman maintains this "lone ranger" mentality, she will find herself frustrated, and constantly wondering why her efforts to become better aren't working.

Women tend to make this mistake when they can't deal with competing personalities. Often this is evident in women who have strong personalities. Instead of agreeing to disagree with others in certain situations, they feel that their opinion is the only one that's important. And anything different from what they believe is just wrong and doesn't even warrant consideration. As a result, the arguing, feuding, and division can occur.

Therefore, instead of celebrating one another by focusing on the big picture of the things they do agree on, they put a magnifying glass on the issues they don't agree on, and then it becomes a major conflict.

I have learned one thing in the past year: Some relationships are just not a "good fit."

Often this is due to competing personalities. And that's okay. There's no rule book stating that you have to become best friends with one specific person.

And if you don't get along with certain people, it doesn't mean that you're a bad person. Your solution is to find someone with whom you do have a good fit and a divine connection.

Women also make the mistake of not having female friends when they don't want to open up their hearts or lives to give or receive help from others.

Sometimes, it's important to realize that working with others is not always about what we can get from connecting with others. It's also about what we can give, and how we can become an asset to one another.

When a woman doesn't connect with the right people, she robs herself of the opportunity to give and ultimately receive from others.

Let me tell you a quick story to illustrate this point...

It's just been in the last few years that I, (Tiffany) have finally been able to extend myself to make close, intimate female friendships.

Because of my past female relationships which tended to be shallow, full of insecurity, and pride, (on both my part and others) I tended to back away from these types of relationships. After a while, I became fearful of reaching out to other women who could complement instead of compete with me.

But I've learned from many of the women I now admire that it's important to have healthy female relationships. So I began to trust God to supply me with good friends with whom I could connect and find a safe place to share my heart.

In fact, I prayed for and spoke into existence my female relationships for years before I actually had them. I prayed that I would have female friends in my life and find people who I could trust to come into my life in an intimate way.

Also, during this time, as I began to take a self-examination of my own life, I began to realize that I didn't need to look for the "perfect friend" who would be just like me. After all, I'm not perfect either.

I just needed to find some sisters who were sincere about following Christ, who were real, and not superficial. (By the way, I hate when people are superficial. Just be real!)

Eventually, as I began to pray, trust God, and observe certain women, I realized that there were actually some women with whom I could connect. Now I have about four good girlfriends whom I love and connect with in very unique ways. I am so glad that I have friends now because they have helped me and challenged me to grow in ways I could not have done on my own.

With these friends, I realize that I don't need to share everything about myself with anyone one of them. And none of them really know each other or are connected. However, each one of them have played an important part in my life, and I in theirs.

What should you do instead?

Consider the following questions…

- Do you have at least one or two good, godly female friends with whom you can hang out with and share your heart?

- Were there some female relationships from your past that have soured your outlook on having female relationships?
- If so, can these relationships be repaired?
- What steps can you take to begin this process?
- Do you struggle with insecurity?
- Do you feel a need to compete with other women?
- Do you have a problem with women when they don't agree 100% with your opinions on certain topics?
- Do you feel like you're the only one who can get the job done?
- Do you look at relationships as a waste of time?
- Do you value female friendships?
- If not, why?

What should you do if you've already made this mistake? How do you fix it?

If you've already fallen into this trap, here's how you get out. Learn to trust again.

You may have experienced some hurtful relationships in your past, but consider this.

By now, you have probably matured and grown a lot since your last relationship with another female. Therefore, you are a different person and you have learned from your mistakes. In many ways, you know what to look for and what to stay away from.

Try again to seek out some friends. Yes, it's a risk, but you'll never find friends if you don't start praying, asking, and seeking them out as God directs you.

Recognize that there is no need to compete with others. In the Kingdom, there's no room for competition.

Why?

Because God has a specific plan for each one of us based on His goals for our lives, our personality, our experiences, our spheres of influence, and everything else.

So even if a woman is in the same type of ministry or business as you, there's no need to feel like you need to "beat her" or "outdo" her because you were created for something unique that only you can do.

Recognize that you are not God, nor are you "Superwoman."

While you may be able to do many things well, you can't do everything effectively all the time. This is where connecting with others comes in. Allow yourself to be vulnerable, even if it only means having a friend who is an accountability partner. No matter how great, focused and destiny-oriented you are, you still need accountability.

How do we prevent making this mistake moving forward?

Here's what you should do to prevent this mistake from happening moving forward...

Have the mentality that you want to begin with a fresh start!

Go to different places to find new friends. Choose friends who are different from you. Just because they don't think or look exactly like you doesn't mean they can't add value to your life.

Find people who are comfortable with the real, authentic you, as well as the parts that are blooming and changing as well.

Remember that you cannot do everything on your own. And also, you will need other women to become your cheerleaders. And you may need to offer your strengths to others as well in the relationship.

Learn to appreciate and value the friends you have today, but understand that these same friends may not be the same ones in your circle years from now. Find people who are secure and comfortable with themselves.

They should give you room to grow and you should give them room to grow as well.

Action Steps for This Chapter

Here's a way you can get even better results by doing things a bit differently...

Recognize that experiencing a few bad relationships does not mean that all of your relationships will turn sour. Consider how you have grown over the years. Start slow and ask a friend out for ice cream, coffee, or lunch, for example.

Get to know people and let them talk to see where they are spiritually and mentally. Don't focus so much on the outward appearances. God chooses people based on their character and so should we, (1 Samuel 16:7.)

Realize that relationships are not just about what you can get from a person, also but what you can offer them.

Recognize that good friendships are worth the investment of time, patience, and love. Also, recognize that life is not all about work and ministry, but about enjoying the harvest of what you've worked so hard for and the things that God has given you.

Our BIGGEST piece of advice moving forward...

Here is my biggest and best piece of advice for you in this area now and moving forward...

Be willing to trust God for new friends. Trust Him to lead you to the friends you need to help carry you to your destiny. Be patient and don't try to force anything. Just let it flow because good friendships take time to develop.

Summary:

Let's summarize:

- Women often make the mistake of not having one or two godly female friends with whom they can become transparent.
- Women tend to make this mistake because they often don't trust other women.
- When women don't have friends, they can end up lonely and unbalanced.
- Recognize that a few bad relationships do not mean that all of your relationships with women will eventually turn sour on you.
- Be willing to trust God to lead you to the friends you need who will carry you to your destiny.
- Be patient and don't try to force anything. Just let it flow because good friendships take time to develop.

Now that we've gotten past the MISTAKE of having female friends, it's time to go over how to avoid NEXT MISTAKE.

MISTAKE #8: THANKS FOR WHAT?

"in everything give thanks; for this is the will of God in Christ Jesus for you."   **1 Thessalonians 5:18**

What is the mistake?

Not being grateful for the things God has already given you.

Simply stated, this mistake occurs when people suffer from ingratitude. They don't thank God for what they currently have.

It also occurs when people want what others have.

Often people fail to recognize the blessings they have and experience on a daily basis. They look for the "big, spectacular" things to occur instead of appreciating the little daily blessings from each day.

For instance, a lady may be lonely and waiting for a husband, but fail to appreciate the positive friendships she currently has.

Or a woman may want a new car, but never learn to thank God for the reliable car that takes her from home to work and church consistently. In addition, she may have a beautiful home, good health, and a faithful husband who loves her and comes home every night. But since she doesn't have the exact car she wants, to her, life sucks!

Wow! How short-sighted is this?

Why is it a mistake?

This is a mistake because God's Word tells us to appreciate and be grateful for what we already have. It's a mistake because ingratitude is a sin, and it hurts God's feelings. It's also a mistake because God wants us to appreciate what we have and not focus on what others have or what we don't have or what we don't have.

God wants to shower us with blessings, but if we don't learn to appreciate what we now have, He may not get too excited about giving us what we ask for later.

What are the consequences of making this mistake and how critical are they?

When people don't thank God for His blessings, they can become frustrated and begin to complain.

Their vision becomes clouded and they fail to see the good things they already have.

When people aren't grateful, they get stuck in life and fail to see God's goodness around them. They mentally hit a dead end because they don't recognize what God can offer them through the things they currently have and what He's willing to give them in the future.

Often this ingratitude can lead people to lose sight of what they have and wrongfully desire or lust for what others have. But the reality is that things are not what they seem to be. And the sad thing is people often become jealous and envious of a mirage – what they THINK someone else has!

When people want what others have, they can become jealous and waste their time focusing on others when they should focus on God. As a result, they can miss hearing God's voice and they end up wasting a lot of time.

Why and when do people tend to make this mistake?

People make these mistakes because they don't recognize how blessed they are or how much God really loves them. While it's not healthy to compare yourself to other people, sometimes when you do see others, you'll recognize that you could be in a worse place.

Ingratitude often kicks in because people become discontent with the things God has already blessed them with.

They're constantly waiting for God to do the "big" things instead of appreciating God for the "little" things in life.

This is a mistake because it hinders you from focusing on the ordered steps God has for you.

People make this mistake when they feel they are entitled to get everything they want. Often people are raised to believe they can have anything they want without doing the hard work to get it or enduring the process of patience and faith.

While God does bless us with things we don't deserve at times because of His grace, He often uses our wants and desires to draw us closer to Him. As we become more like God by spending time with Him, we learn to enjoy being in His presence. The blessings we do get then become by-products of the process we went through to grow in Christ.

Ingratitude occurs when God doesn't do things the way people want Him to do it. People struggle with this when they don't understand the beauty of thanksgiving. They make this mistake when they don't understand who they are in Christ. Also, not understanding God's unconditional love and their value, can cause people to focus less on Christ and more on getting stuff.

As a result, when they don't get exactly what they want, they get frustrated because they put their value in stuff and not Christ. Then they suffer from low self-esteem because they allowed stuff to make them feel more significant than their undying relationship with Christ.

Let us tell you a quick story to illustrate this point...

I (Tiffany) grew up as an only child. My parents often gave me whatever I wanted, so I grew up with a sense of entitlement. As a result, I never really learned to appreciate the blessings that God had given me until I became grown.

I often never had a problem getting a job, doing well, or getting what I wanted because of the strong relationships my parents built with their friends and colleagues. But as I grew older I faced a ton of hardships, including rejection, unemployment, foreclosure, church hurt, and many other calamities.

I was stripped of everything that was familiar and comfortable to me, and that hurt, both mentally and emotionally!

I didn't have much left except my marriage, my family, my health, and my salvation. I began to realize that having these things was worthy of my praise and worship to God.

It felt like I was coming up out of a heap of ashes. And God was there waiting for me to grab His hand so He could lead me out of this heap of ashes. I had lost a lot, but I still had enough left for God to work with! And fortunately, I learned how I could rebuild from there.

When I began to realize the blessings I had left, I began to thank God for these things, and I recognized that the "little" things God had given me were more important than anything.

Questions to Consider

Consider the following questions…

- Have I been ungrateful? If so, why?

- What "small things" can I thank God for today?

- What can I miss if I continue to focus on what I don't have?

- Am I jealous of someone? If so, why? What do they have that I want?

- Are the things I want from God really what He wants me to have?

- If I have lost anything, what's left that I can still thank God for?

What should you do if you've already made this mistake? How do you fix it?

When you go through a frustrating or hurtful situation, refuse to focus solely on what you have lost, but rather concentrate on what you have gained.

For you, it may be patience, self-control, compassion, or any other positive traits that you may have overlooked.

If you've already made this mistake, you can repent and confess it to God.

You need to begin thanking God for what you currently have. Even if you've lost a lot, you can thank God for the good things you have left.

Learn to understand the power of gratitude. Begin to recognize what God has blessed you with already.

Start the journey of learning who you are in Christ, so you can recognize His plan for your life. You need to focus on what God is doing for you right now!

How do we prevent making this mistake moving forward?

Here's what you should do to prevent this mistake from happening moving forward...

Take quiet time to recognize what you currently have left. Begin to speak words of thanksgiving and adoration to God for these things.

To avoid jealousy, begin to compliment those who have what you want. It causes you to encourage others and switches the focus from you back onto God and His goodness.

Note, there's nothing wrong with having expectations and looking forward to more of God's blessings and favor. But you must keep your goals and desires in the right perspective.

Action Steps for This Chapter

Here's an awesome tool that will help you get the results you're looking for...

You can create a thanksgiving journal. It doesn't need to be expensive. You can use a regular notebook or a composition book. Or you can go fancy and get a colorful, hard bound journal.

In this journal, write down at least three things a day that you are grateful for.

You can put these things into categories. For example, you can take a week to write down three things about you family. You may have a parent, husband, or kids in your life you are grateful for. If everyone is healthy, well, or at least have improved, that's something to thank God for. Write it down!

Or there may be some people in your life who have already passed away, but made a strong impact in your life. Thank God for how they helped you to grow.

You can even thank God for your own health and strength. After all, everyone does not have their health or strength.

You can thank Him for a place to stay, your education, or the things He has delivered you from. For us, we can write a list of the sins He set us free from.

Our BIGGEST piece of advice moving forward...

Here is our biggest and best piece of advice for you in this area now and moving forward...

Learn to thank God for the little things and appreciate what you currently have. As a result, God will bless you with the "bigger" things in due time.

Summary:

Let's summarize:

- Ingratitude occurs when people don't thank God for what they currently have.

- Being ungrateful is a mistake because it's a sin and breaks God's heart.

- To avoid jealousy, begin to compliment those who have what you want.

- When people begin to discover who they are in Christ they can avoid ingratitude and recognize His strategic plan for their lives.

- You need to focus on what God is doing for you instead of what you THINK He is doing for others.

- Create a thanksgiving journal to write down the blessings you have in your possession right now.

- Whatever you focus on will continue to grow in your life, so concentrate on what you have left.

- There's nothing wrong with praying and asking God for more, but you should be grateful for what you already have in your life.

Now that we've covered how to avoid the MISTAKE of ingratitude, it's time to move on to the NEXT CHAPTER.

CHAPTER 9: OOPS! I MISCOUNTED...

"For which of you, intending to build a tower, does not sit down first and count the cost, whether he has enough to finish it..." Luke 14:28

What is the mistake?

Making quick, impulsive decisions without considering the outcome.

This mistake happens when people make hasty, self-centered decisions instead of counting the cost and considering the consequences first. This can be disastrous!

When it comes to making major decisions, it's important to get advice from sources other than yourself. Not consulting God first through prayer often causes a person to make the wrong decisions. In addition, not seeking godly counsel from God-centered friends and/or experts can cause problems as well.

Note, when I say God-centered "decisions," I don't mean trivial things such as choosing what outfit to wear for the day or what restaurant to choose. Instead, major decisions refer to the ones that will affect you, or others around you, and/or your purpose. Examples include:

- Who you should marry
- Choosing the right profession
- What school to attend
- Whether or not to refinance your home

Why is it a mistake?

Every day we are required to make choices: some big and some small.

For instance, we must decide where to go, how early to leave for an appointment, and what we will have for lunch. While most of these things are not life-altering circumstances, there are some choices that can affect us for a lifetime and those around us.

It's a mistake not to seek God's guidance through prayer because He wants to be first in every decision you make.

In Revelation 3:20, Jesus says "Behold, I stand at the door and knock. If anyone hears My voice and opens the door, I will come into him and dine with him, and he with Me."

He wants to be at the decision-making tables of our hearts. He wants to hear your concerns and the decisions you make. And He wants to influence your decisions instead of you making the wrong choices and going down the wrong path.

Often when we make a decision on our own without godly guidance, we act from a one-dimensional perspective, and we fail to see the big picture.

We often see what we want to see and not what we need to see when it comes to making decisions. When you don't get counsel from godly people, you may fail to see your decisions from the proper perspective. You may miss the expertise that could help you in making a sound decision.

What are the consequences of making this mistake and how critical are they?

When you fail to count the cost of your decisions before you make them, you could end up in a very bad situation.

When you make decisions without God's guidance and direction you could go farther away from God's plans for your life. As a result, this could lead you to disappointment and frustration because you're in a place that you were not created to be in. In addition, your decision could lead you down a path of delay and even destruction which could take months, if not years to deal with and overcome.

When you fail to consult friends and/or experts in your decision making, you could fail to see the truth in your situation. And you may even have a false sense of security because you didn't look at the negative consequences. You only saw what you wanted to see.

Why and when do people tend to make this mistake?

Pride is the main factor.

People often think they have life all figured out. Often they become resolute in their decisions, and they don't want to be held accountable for their decisions. They already have a plan in mind, and they don't want anyone or anything to "mess it up" or "throw them off."

Often they have tried to consult God but weren't patient enough to wait to hear from Him. Or they don't believe He will respond. Maybe they know the decision they're making is not the right one, and they don't really want God's opinion.

Sometimes God takes a longer time to give us an answer. And when the answer takes too long to come, we move on to our "option B", whether we have peace about it or not. We convince ourselves that this is the right plan, we make preparations for it, and we execute the plan despite God's red flags not to go further in the plan.

We don't trust God because there have been times when He didn't give us exactly what we wanted in the past, so we exclude God from the process.

In some cases, we may consult family or friends, but we still think the decision we've made is right. We may not value our friend's opinion enough because they think they have it all figured out for themselves.

Also, our friends and family have often led us down the wrong path before so we don't want deal with them anymore.

People tend to make this mistake when they have already made a decision, and they don't want to think about the bad consequences. They are so hopeful and optimistic that they really want to believe that everything will turn out for the best.

People often take their friends and family for granted, although these people have traveled the road on which they are going. We'll be the first to tell you, there are some family members and friends who we would never ask to give us advice. But there are some whose opinions we value because they understand the path we're attempting to walk.

There are times when we have to make a decision solely based on God's leading. But we have to know it's God and not our flesh.

Let us tell you a quick story to illustrate this point...

A simple example is marriage.

Let's call her Lisa. She's a Christian who serves in the church. She loved God more than anything…until she met someone.

Lisa connected with the wrong man. His name was Jason. When Lisa first started dating Jason, she enjoyed his company, and before you knew it, she was in love. Jason liked Lisa, but he really wasn't ready for marriage.

But eventually, Lisa kept pressuring Jason to get married.

She eventually got engaged to Jason. But when Lisa's pastor recommended that she and Jason take pre-marital counseling, she refused because she thought she knew everything about Jason. And he didn't want to go to counseling because he thought it was too invasive.

Despite the warnings God gave Lisa, she married Jason not too long after their engagement.

Since Lisa was so in love with this man, she couldn't see any of his flaws when they were dating, especially his anger problem. Jason seemed like the perfect man. In her mind, Lisa knew that once they were married, purchased their own home, and began their new life together, Jason's anger problem would get better, so she thought.

In fact, Lisa's ultimate plan was to "change" Jason once she married him.

But after the marriage, she quickly realized that she could not change Jason. In fact, Jason's anger escalated to a shove, then a slap in the face, and ultimately separation due to full-blown domestic violence.

After 3 years of a tumultuous marriage, a baby, and major debt Lisa is now frustrated, lonely, and bitter, because she finally realized that she had connected with the wrong man.

Lisa's friends tried to tell her that Jason was no good, but she kept on her blinders. Marriage was a life-changing decision because it affected Lisa's finances, her heart, and even her lifestyle.

All along, God showed Lisa snapshots of Jason's real side, but Lisa failed to heed the warnings.

Lisa made the decision to press through with her heart.

It's not wrong to listen to your heart, however, when it's not in tune with God, your heart can lead you in the wrong direction.

What questions should you consider?

Consider the following questions

- What is the decision you need to make?

- What choices do you have?

- Is it a decision that needs to be made quickly or do you have some time to think about it?

- What are your motives for making the decision?

- Will your decision only benefit you or will it benefit others for the glory of God?

- How will this decision you make affect those closest to you in the long run?

- Have you prayed about your decision?

- Have you talked to a trusted godly friend who has your interest at heart?

- Have you talked with someone who has a high level of success in this particular area?

What should you do if you've already made this mistake? How do you fix it?

If you've already fallen into this trap, here's how you get out.

Remember, don't beat yourself up for your mistakes because you are not your mistakes. Your mistakes cannot define you unless you allow them to do so. God can fix any mistake you have made.

Take some time to think about where you are. Just get quiet before God and don't try to fix it yet. You may need time to readjust, reboot, and refocus your thoughts and your priorities.

Confess to God for not consulting Him about your decision first. Ask Him to help you.

While God may not be pleased with your decision, He still loves you, and He wants to bring you out of the mess you're in. Don't be afraid or ashamed to ask Him for help. He's not like people who will "write you off" if you don't do what they tell you to do the first time.

Ask God to lead you to some people who can help you and redirect you on the right path. Write their names down and write why you think they could benefit you in your decision making.

Consider their personality styles. Consider if they will offer you mercy especially if they tried to offer you advice before. You don't need anyone kicking you while you're down. At this point, you need some sound advice and compassion!

How do we prevent making this mistake moving forward?

Here's what you should do to prevent this mistake from happening moving forward...

Pray, pray, pray before making any other major decisions. Major decisions include things such as:

- Choosing a new job
- Who you should date
- Who you should marry
- Whether you should move or not
- Where you should move
- Buying a house or a car
- Any other life-altering decisions

Ask yourself if the decision you're making lines up with where God is trying to take you. If you're unsure, then you need to spend some quiet time to see where He wants you to go.

Think about the people in your life. Do you have a friend, a mentor, or a coach who can give you some guidance and accountability for the decisions you're about to make?

If you need coaching, please contact us at **info@RelationshipMissionaries.com**.

Action Steps for This Chapter

Here's a way you can get even better results by doing things a bit differently...

Your greatest resource is the Bible. This is God's love letter to you. In it, God will give you instruction in the form of Biblical principles.

Time is one of your greatest tools. You need time to consider and think about "the good, the bad, and the ugly" (results) of the decisions you will make in the future. Write down your thoughts in your journal.

Jesus even says to count the cost. Make sure you have what it takes to start, finish, and maintain while you're waiting to make your decision in the "middle" of your waiting.

Understand that the "middle" is the toughest part of any project. The beginning is exciting. The end is your finish line, the completed task. But in the middle, you have a lot of distractions, bumps, hindrances, and doubts.

When you take time to think about these things, you may come to the conclusion that you either don't need to make that decision for the time being, or you may decide to proceed with the decision. But when you give it time, you give yourself time to think. You also need to give God time to move on your behalf, one way or another.

When time is of the essence, you have the ability to say no. If someone is pressing you for a decision immediately, in whatever it is, whether it's for a new job, a move, or marriage, you need to understand that this may be the type of circumstance you'll be dealing with long-term.

We've learned our lesson of counting the cost the hard way through a series of mistakes and loss. But now, we know better when making major decisions. For instance, when something moves too quickly, and we're being pressured to make a decision too soon, we question if it's the right choice for us at that time.

Our BIGGEST piece of advice moving forward...

Here is my biggest and best piece of advice for you in this area now and moving forward...

Always take time to consider the cost of the decision you're about to make by seeking God's guidance, giving it time, and receiving godly counsel.

Summary:

Let's summarize:

- Failing to count the cost from the decisions you've made can be disastrous.

- When you make decisions without God's guidance and direction you could be going farther away from God's plans for your life.

- Take some time to think about where you are. Just get quiet before God and don't try to fix it yet. You need time to readjust, reboot, and refocus your thoughts.

- Pray, pray, pray before making any major decisions.

- Your greatest resource is the Bible, which is God's love letter to you. It will give you the proper guidance in making serious life decisions.

- You are not your mistakes and God can fix anything!

Now that we've covered how to avoid the CURRENT MISTAKE, it's time to move on to how to avoid the NEXT MISTAKE.

CHAPTER 10: TAG, YOU'RE IT!

"Then the Lord God said to the woman, 'What is this that you have done?' And the woman said, 'The serpent beguiled and deceived me...'"
Genesis 3:13 (MSG)

What is the mistake?

Playing the blame game.

Often in life, we make excuses for our failures.

We adopt a victim mentality, and as a result, we refuse to take responsibility when we mess up. Then we blame other people for our sins, failures, and shortcomings.

The first "Blame Game" instance occurred in Genesis 3 with Adam and Eve. God gave Adam specific instructions: Don't eat of the tree of knowledge of good and evil. (Genesis 2:16-17)

Adam made a decision to disobey God, and as a result, sin came into the world. But instead of accepting responsibility for what he did, Adam blamed Eve.

Where did Adam take responsibility or show leadership in this situation?

And then Eve blamed the serpent, who was the devil.

Wow! Even back then, people said, "The devil made me do it!"

Why is it a mistake?

It's a mistake because making excuses is a sign of insecurity and immaturity.

When we refuse to take responsibility, this also demonstrates pride. It pushes the burden off of us and puts it on another person.

The problem is that blaming others does not help you to deal with the real issue -- you!

What are the consequences of making this mistake and how critical are they?

When you make excuses for your failures, you avoid looking at your problems, and you don't allow yourself to get to the root of your issues. Your problems and issues keep looming over your head. And often times you'll end up dealing with the same types of people and issues until you decide to change your attitude and approach.

Also, when you choose not to take responsibility, you stay stuck, and you begin to feel sorry for yourself. You begin to wallow in self-pity and you become addicted to pain as you nurse your wounds, waiting for the next big event, thing, or person to save you from your pit.

When you blame others, you also deplete your ability to change your situation, and you place your destiny and power into the hands of another person.

Why and when do people tend to make this mistake?

They need an escape, a way out of taking responsibility for their wrong decisions and actions.

People make excuses due to procrastination and no true desire to change their situation for the better. Procrastination causes you to stay stuck.

You say you want to change and you may even know what it takes, but you choose not to do it. This lack of taking action could be due to hurt, frustration, and even burnout.

You're tired of trying, so you just…stop!

Many people lose passion for life and let go of their goals.

And in many cases, people don't want to do what it takes to make a real change. They will often complain that it's too hard and too much work. It takes them out of their comfort zone.

People tend to make this mistake when they...

They make excuses when they have been caught doing wrong or when their bad decisions have led them to a place of failure. Everyone sees their failure, and they can't even explain their way out. So instead of admitting to failure, they look for excuses and people to blame in hope that it will take the spotlight off of them.

When the pressure is too great, they tend to crumble and try to push the blame onto someone else.

They refuse to take responsibility when they can pass the blame onto someone else. That's an easier route for them to take.

This can especially occur with people in leadership. As a leader, there's a major weight to carry. As a leader, you represent other people and their successes as well as their failures. For this reason, the leader will be required to take responsibility for his/her followers.

When something goes wrong, effective leadership requires a willingness to say, "I did it, but I will do whatever it takes to improve…"

Then as a leader, you go to the actual source of the problem to see how you can help to change or work towards improvement.

Even if you are not a leader, as a Christian, you represent Christ.

People will automatically look to you for direction and guidance, and to some people you will be the only "Christ" they will ever see. When you do something wrong, admit it because if you don't, they will judge Christ based on your actions. And if you're having a bad day, and make some mistakes, but refuse to admit it, you could become a stumbling block to that person and maybe even miss out on your blessing.

Let us tell you a quick story to illustrate this point...

A simple example would be running late for an appointment.

Sandra has a job interview. Her rent, her car payment, and her food supply all depend on her getting this job. She arrives at the interview ten minutes late.

Sandra's prospective boss, Lacy, (though impressed with Sandra's resume and phone interview) glares at Sandra as they sit down. Lacy has a strong, "take no junk" attitude and work ethic.

"Is there a reason why you were late?" asked the interviewer with a raised eyebrow.

Casually, Sandra responds, as she sweeps her hair to the back of her ear, "Well...traffic was slow," she grins, "Apparently there was an accident. And it was hard to find a parking once I got here. Not to mention, I had to pay for parking. Do you offer a reimbursement for this?"

"The nerve of this woman," thinks Lacy as she ignores Sandra's last statement and proceeds with the interview process.

"Sandra, why did you only spend 6 months at your last job?"

Sandra responds, "My boss had a <u>major</u> attitude problem. She never trained me, and plus she never gave me a chance to ask questions. She was negative and expected me to solve all of her problems..."

The truth was that Sandra ran late and she (more times than not), took 45 minutes on her lunch break when she was only allotted 30 minutes. Also, she spent a lot of time on Facebook when she should have been working on her projects.

In this situation, Sandra failed to take responsibility for her tardiness to the interview. And she failed to acknowledge her contribution to her termination from her previous job. Instead, she blamed other people namely her ex-boss.

As a result, Sandra probably will lose the opportunity of getting hired for this new job. She will lose her apartment, her car, and will probably be forced to move back into her mother's home!

And then she will blame Lacy for not hiring her for the job!

Questions to Consider?

Consider the following questions…

- How did I get to where I am now?

- Do I make excuses for my failures and mistakes?

- What can I do to make better decisions?

- Do I have a problem with procrastination?

- What are some of the fears that keep me from taking action?

- What hinders me from holding myself accountable?

- Is there someone I can reach out to for accountability?

- Who do I blame for my mistakes and problems?

- Do I need to apologize to the people I have blamed in the past for my problems and mistakes?

- What can I do to change my habit of blaming others?

What should you do if you've already made this mistake? How do you fix it?

If you've already fallen into this trap, here's how you get out.

Look for an accountability partner.

Consider people who have a heart for God and know you well. Refer back to the section(s) on how to find good, godly friends who can help you to grow.

Prayerfully consider asking one or two of these people to become your accountability partners. These people should have your best interest at heart. Also, the people you choose should not be intimidated by you or the things you have. They should not be scared to correct you when you are wrong or tell you no when you are going down the wrong path.

If you can't find a trusted friend, I recommend you hire a life coach.

The purpose of a life coach is not to deal with your past issues. A life coach's job is to learn about your goals and ask you questions that will help you to create a life strategy. They can help you to figure out how to reach those goals.

Life coaches want to look at your present so they can help to propel you into your future and fulfill your God-given destiny.

Also, life coaches specialize in many areas, including organization, business, relationships, fitness, etc.

For instance, we are life coaches who specialize in relationships coaching.

I (Tiffany) specialize in helping women to improve their marriage and dating relationships. As a couple, we work with other married and engaged couples to help them to strengthen communication and work through the issues that threaten to destroy their relationship. We also offer our clients practical steps and tips for growth and improvement as they pursue their purpose.

For more information on the relationship coaching services we provide, go to:

http://www.RelationshipMissionaries.com.

Lastly, from this day, make the decision to stop blaming people for what you have done wrong.

How do we prevent making this mistake moving forward?

Here's what you should do to prevent this mistake from moving forward...

Get to know yourself.

What or who do you turn to when stress hits? Food, chocolate, your best friend, or a man?

Figure out why you do the things you do. I recommend you take a personality test to find out the "method to your madness" when it comes to decision making.

One of the most effective tests is called the DISC personality test. It helps you to recognize your personality, and it also enables you to recognize personality traits in others so you can deal with them more effectively.

To learn more about the DISC personality test, go to: http://relationshipmissionaries.com/discpersonalitytypesvideo/

The DISC personality test will help you to recognize how you react under pressure and how to improve.

Taking and getting the results of your personality test can help you to see why you fail to take responsibility in certain areas.

Whatever you do, keep your power!

When you blame others, you give them the power to control your destiny. Recognize that your power comes from God and He gives it to you in order to fulfill the plan He has for your life.

Action Steps for This Chapter

Here's a way you can get even better results by doing things a bit differently...

Take the DISC personality test. When you contact us at info@RelationshipMissionaries.com, let us know you read this book and once you decide to take the test, **you will receive 10% off of your test.**

This test will help you to learn more about your personality style.

In addition, if you can't find a trusted friend, I recommend you seek out a professional life coach. They will help you to get closer to your destiny by helping you to assess where you are and then help you to reach your goals.

A life coach will hold you accountable and give you a strategic plan for success in certain areas of your life where you have had struggles.

If you are interested we would love to coach you. You can start with our FREE 20-minute session. You can:

- Go to RelationshipMissionaries.com
- Go to: Relationship Coaching or Life Purpose Coaching
- Fill out the form
- Someone will contact you shortly

Also, as you grow, get a journal to document your growth and the changes you've seen over a period of time. Go back to this journal after a few months so you can celebrate your progress!

Our BIGGEST piece of advice moving forward...

Here is my biggest and best piece of advice for you in this area now and moving forward...

Don't remain stuck in your mess!

Make the decision to take action and responsibility for your actions so you can take your God-given power back, make a difference, and fulfill your destiny and purpose.

Summary:

Let's summarize:

- Often in life, we make excuses for our failures.

- People don't want to do what it takes to change because they think it's too hard and too much work.

- Change takes people out of their comfort zone.

- When the pressure is too great, they tend to crumble and try to push the blame onto someone else.

- Take the DISC personality test. This test will help you to learn more about your personality style. It also helps you to deal with other people properly.

- Find some trusted friends who will hold you accountable.

- If you can't find a few trusted, close godly friends to hold you accountable, hire a professional life coach who will hold you accountable and help you to reach your goals.

CONCLUSION

Congrats! You have come to the last stretch of this book.

Now that you understand the mistakes Christian women make when pursuing their purpose and how to fix them, we want to share our personal checklist to make sure you avoid these mistakes and get "unstuck."

Here is a checklist that contains specific questions to ask and actions to take to make sure you avoid these mistakes.

Below, you'll find your personal checklist. Follow this checklist and you'll know you'll be covered:

1) Do I have a journal to record my questions, goals, places of growth, and discoveries about pursuing my purpose?

2) Am I 100% convinced that God created me for a specific purpose regardless of where I am now or where I came from?

3) Do I realize that my purpose is birthed from my passions, talents, skills, and experiences, (good or bad)?

4) Do I recognize that God is madly in love with me and He loves me regardless of what I've done, what I look like, or who I am?

5) Am I willing to identify, deal with, and overcome the dark places in my life to pursue my purpose?

6) Do I believe that the Bible is God's inerrant Word that guides me and gives me direction for living and discovering my life purpose?

7) Do I ever take quiet time to hear what God is saying to me?

8) Am I willing to spend time reading and studying God's Word on a consistent basis so I can get to know Him better?

9) Is there anyone or any situation in my life that I need to forgive and release?

10) Do I need to forgive myself?

11) What are my biggest fears? Are they hindering me from pursuing my purpose?

12) Do I have any good, godly female friends who care about me? If not, why?

13) Are my relationships with these females healthy, and do they encourage me so I can pursue my purpose?

14) Do I encourage my friends to walk in and pursue their destiny?

15) Are there any women who God is leading me to connect with?

16) Do I struggle with ingratitude? If so, why?

17) Do I make God-centered decisions or impulsive decisions on a consistent basis?

18) Do I talk to God about major decisions and wait to hear His response?

19) Who do I talk to when I need to make major decisions?

20) Does this advice help or hurt me?

21) Do I take responsibility for my failures or do I often blame others for them?

22) Do I have an accountability partner, such as a godly, unbiased friend or a life coach?

Final Thoughts

The #1 thing we wish someone would have told us was that God created us for a specific purpose.

Although we sensed this, even as children, we didn't know exactly what this meant.

And because of that, we both wasted a lot of time with the wrong people, doing things we had no business doing!

Does this sound familiar?

With this in mind, we're sure you have a few of these mistakes you wish you could correct. But we don't want you to overwhelm yourself trying to fix every mistake you've made all at once.

We suggest you choose three of these mistakes you need to correct and fix them first.

We recommend you choose the three easiest ones first, the three you just know you need to tackle. This will help you to build some momentum and feel like a champion once you deal with them.

Then choose three more and fix those next.

We hope you enjoyed this. We know that by paying attention to these 10 mistakes, you will improve, grow and get closer to your ultimate purpose.

Next Steps

Your next steps are quick and to the point. Avoid these mistakes at all costs.

Use this checklist to ensure you're doing the best to reach your destiny. Always strive to give it your all 100% of the time, but remember that even your best is still limited without the help and power of Christ when pursuing God's purpose in life.

Most importantly, you need to keep seeking the power and presence of the Holy Spirit through prayer to help you through this process. God will give you the grace you need to press on when you feel like you can't do anything else.

He is the Source of every good thing you do. And because He gave you a purpose, He will give you the power to fulfill it.

Lastly, listen to God's voice and never settle for mediocrity when it comes to pursuing your purpose. You deserve better because you are God's masterpiece and He created you for greatness.

MEET DEXTER AND TIFFANY GODFREY

 Dexter and Tiffany Godfrey enjoy training, speaking to, and coaching individuals, churches, business professionals, and married couples on the benefits of doing life based on God's principles.

Their goal is to help people to start from where they are and pick up the broken pieces of their lives, so they can end at the finish line to fulfill the destiny and purpose of God for their lives.

About Dexter

Dexter is a well-known speaker, coach, and trainer, who is highly sought after by churches, CEO's, and companies across the country.

Dexter has trained various sales professionals, managers, and CEO's in the areas of real estate, customer service, marriage, and other relationship-based fields.

His engaging, yet practical style has earned him invitations as keynote speaker in various faith-based and business arenas. In addition to writing many articles and books, Dexter is the bestselling author of the book, *It's Who You Know: Top 12 Mistakes People Make Building Relationships...And How to Avoid Them.*

As a **John Maxwell certified speaker and coach**, Dexter equips people in the professional arena to take their careers, businesses, and ministries to a new, and "out of the box" level.

He also enjoys reading, golfing, and basketball.

About Tiffany

Tiffany is a women's relationship coach, specializing in the areas of marriage, dating, and pre-marriage. She is also a bestselling author and speaker.

Her ultimate goal is to help women to pursue their relationship with Christ so they can overcome their fears, their past, and their frustrations, in order to pursue their destiny.

Tiffany is the author of various books and articles. Her latest eBook is called, *Relationship Coaching Tools: The 7 Types of Relationships & 50 Intense Relationship Coaching Questions That Will Save You Time, Money, Frustration, and Heartbreak!*

In her spare time, she enjoys reading, volleyball, and writing.

As a Team

Dexter and Tiffany have been married for almost 17 years and from this union they have 2 sons.

Through **RelationshipMissionaries.com**, Dexter and Tiffany connect to combine their gifts and experiences to coach, train, and equip men and women to build both their personal and business relationships for their success and God's glory.

Through their relationship with Christ and life lessons, Dexter and Tiffany share with other people who can relate to their enthusiasm and real-life stories.

ADDITIONAL RESOURCES BY DEXTER AND TIFFANY

Dexter

- *It's Who You Know: Top 12 Mistakes People Make Building Relationships...And How to Avoid Them*
- *Fearless Success (It's Up To You): 45 Fearless Success Tips to Put Into Action For Immediate Results*
- *The Top 10 Real Estate Investing Tips and Tricks Every Real Estate Agent and Broker Needs To Know*

Tiffany

- *Relationship Coaching Tools: The 7 Types of Relationships & 50 Intense Relationship Coaching Questions That Will Save You Time, Money, Frustration, and Heartbreak!*
- *The Top 12 Mistakes Married Women Make...And How to Avoid Them!*
- *Is Marriage a Joke? How the Christian Woman Can Kick Off Communication In Marriage Without Causing More Marriage Problems!*